NEW DIREC
IN JUDICIAL

SEVEN DAY LOAN

This book is to be returned on
or before the date stamped below

UNIVERSITY OF PLYMOUTH

PLYMOUTH LIBRARY

Tel: (01752) 232323

This book is subject to recall if required by another reader
Books may be renewed by phone
CHARGES WILL BE MADE FOR OVERDUE BOOKS

AUSTRALIA
The Law Book Company Ltd.
Sydney: Melbourne: Brisbane: Perth

CANADA
The Carswell Company Ltd.
Toronto: Calgary: Vancouver: Ottawa

INDIA
N. M. Tripathi Private Ltd.
Bombay
and
Eastern Law House Private Ltd.
Calcutta

M.P.P. House
Bangalore

ISRAEL
Steimatzky's Agency Ltd.
Jerusalem: Tel Aviv: Haifa

PAKISTAN
Pakistan Law House
Karachi

NEW DIRECTIONS IN JUDICIAL REVIEW

CURRENT LEGAL PROBLEMS

Edited by

J. L. Jowell, M.A., LL.M, Barrister

Professor of Public Law, Dean, Faculty of Laws,
University College London

and

D. Oliver, M.A., Barrister

Senior Lecturer, University College London

London
Stevens & Sons
1988

Published in 1988
by Stevens & Sons Limited now of
South Quay Plaza, 183 Marsh Wall, London.
Laserset by P.B. Computer Typesetting, Pickering, N. Yorks.
Printed in Great Britain

Reprinted 1990

British Library Cataloguing in Publication Data

Jowell, J.
New directions in judicial review
administration. — (Current legal problems).
1. Great Britain. Public administration.
Decision making. Judicial review
I. Title II. Oliver, D. III. Series
344.102′66

ISBN 0–420–47800–0

CONTENTS

CURRENT LEGAL PROBLEMS SPECIAL ISSUES

Company Law in Change, ed. B. Pettet
Essays in Family Law, ed. M. D. A. Freeman
Medicine, Ethics and the Law, ed. M. D. A. Freeman
New Directions in Judicial Review, eds. J. L. Jowell, D. Oliver
New Foundations for Insurance Law, ed. F. D. Rose
Recent Tax Problems, ed. J. Dyson

TABLE OF CASES

TABLE OF STATUTES

Introduction

JEFFREY JOWELL AND DAWN OLIVER

The recent growth of administrative law without doubt constitutes the most significant development in English common law over the past decade. Rapid development of that kind however does not easily permit considered reflection about the extent of the expanded scope of the principles of judicial review and the definition of its limits. This collection of essays selects five issues which pose urgent challenges to administrative law and which are in need of critical evaluation. These issues are: the public/private law distinction; the extension of the range of authorities that are subject to judicial review; the evolving doctrine about the protection of legitimate expectations; the principle of proportionality as a ground for review; and the increasing judicial supervision of the policy-making process.

Since the House of Lords' decision in *O'Reilly* v. *Mackman*[1] the courts have had to establish boundaries between public and private law. Michael Beloff Q.C., in his article on "The boundaries of judicial review" considers some of the "no man's land" where it is not clear whether judicial review is available. This territory includes the activities of domestic bodies or tribunals and self-regulatory bodies, and the "private" lives of "public" bodies, including employment and contract compliance. The ambit of *O'Reilly* v. *Mackman* is discussed, together with the variety of exceptions to that doctrine that have already been established as a result of the House of Lords' decision in *Wandsworth* v. *Winder*[2] and other cases. The present state of the law is, Michael Beloff suggests, unclear and unsatisfactory and possible solutions to the problems posed by the *O'Reilly* decision are considered. These include the overruling of *O'Reilly* v. *Mackman*, the possibility of assimilating the procedures in public and private law by extending the requirement for leave to all actions against 'public bodies', and a radical statutory reform of public law remedies.

The decision of the Court of Appeal in *R.* v. *Panel on Takeovers and Mergers, Ex p. Datafin*[3] expands the class of bodies that may be subjected to judicial review under Order 53 of the Rules of the Supreme Court. In his paper on "What is a public authority for the purposes of judicial review?" David Pannick examines the case law on this important and somewhat uncertain topic. It seems that judicial review will lie against the university Visitor and the Civil Service Appeal Board, but it is by no means clear whether organisations such as the BBC, or regulatory bodies in the field of sport are subject to a supervisory jurisdiction, whether in public or private law. David Pannick also considers the grounds on which the court may refuse, as it did in the *Datafin* case, to exercise its supervisory jurisdiction over a body that is a "public authority." These bodies may engage in "private" activity which is not subject to judicial review, in employment and contracting for example. They may also be immune from review in making commercial or managerial decisions, or "non-justiciable" decisions on matters such as defence and foreign affairs.

Patrick Elias in his paper on "Legitimate expectation and judicial review" analyses a number of recent cases in which the courts have given protection to the "legitimate expectations" of applicants for judicial review. The concept was first introduced by Lord Denning in *Schmidt* v. *Secretary of State for Home Affairs*[4] in 1969, and has been developed in a number of cases since then, most notably by Lord Diplock in the *G.C.H.Q.*[5] case. Lord Diplock's analysis is, Patrick Elias suggests, open to criticism for failing to distinguish between legitimate expectations, which attract protection because of the conduct of the decision-maker, and rights and interests, which are protected independently, and regardless of the conduct of the decision-maker. Lord Diplock's speech seems to imply that mere interests are not entitled to the protection of judicial review unless they were created by the conduct of the decision-maker, and this is not consistent with other cases on the protection of interests such as *R.* v. *Secretary of State for Transport, Ex p. Greater London Council.*[6]

Legitimate expectations may be procedural, as in *Attorney General of Hong Kong* v. *Ng Yuen Shiu*[7] and the *Liverpool Taxi*[8] decision; or substantive, as in *St. Germain*[9] and *Asif Khan.*[10] The protection given to legitimate expectations will normally be procedural, consisting of a duty to consult or listen to representations. But, as was seen in the *G.C.H.Q.* affair, the right to protection of legitimate or reasonable expectations may yield to the requirements of national security. Where a legitimate expectation is entitled to protection the courts have gone further than mere procedural protection and actually extended substantive protection to the expectation.

In the *G.C.H.Q.* case Lord Diplock attempted to categorise the grounds for judicial review. In addition to the heads of illegality, irrationality and procedural impropriety, he hinted at the possibility of the development of an additional ground, "proportionality." In their paper on "Proportionality: neither novel nor dangerous" Jeffrey Jowell and Anthony Lester Q.C. trace the pedigree of this concept in German, French and European Community law and in the jurisprudence of the European Convention on Human Rights. They show that proportionality is also a general principle of English law, as has been demonstrated in public law cases like *R. v. Barnsley M.D.C, Ex p. Hook*[11] and, more recently, the *Wheeler*[12] and *Assegai*[13] cases. Proportionality also has a long pedigree in criminal law, planning law and other areas, in private as well as public law, although often passing under other names. The authors argue that English administrative law would now be strengthened if the principle of proportionality were explicitly recognised.

The policy-making process has attracted considerable attention from students of politics and public administration, and relatively little from lawyers, who have concentrated on decision-making and administrative action. The House of Lords decisions in *Bushell v. Secretary of State for the Environment*[14]; on cross-examination designed to challenge policy-making methodology, and in *re Findlay*,[15] on the Home Secretary's change of policy on awarding parole to prisoners, appeared to indicate a reluctance on the part of the courts to lay down any requirements of consultation or fact-gathering in the policy-making process. Dawn Oliver, in her paper on "The courts and the policy-making process" suggests however that it is generally only where policy is overwhelmingly a matter of value judgment, or where an appropriate procedure is not possible, that the courts are reluctant to lay down a policy-making process. In the *Brent*[16] and *British Oxygen*[17] cases and others the courts have indicated that where legitimate expectations, rights or interests are affected by a change of policy a prudent process and consultation with representatives of affected groups should take place. The courts therefore appear to be ready to concern themselves with the policy-making process, which is a significant new direction in administrative law.

Each essay in this collection, while primarily addressing one of the specific issues described above, also speaks to the general scope, the limits and the current mood of judicial review. We trust that the collection as a whole, through its mix of description and critical evaluation, will assist the difficult task facing courts reviewing administrative authorities in the years to come.

University College London

January 1988

Jeffrey Jowell

Dawn Oliver

Notes

[1] [1983] 2 A.C. 237.
[2] [1985] A.C. 461.
[3] [1987] Q.B. 815.
[4] [1969] 2 Ch. 149.
[5] *Council of Civil Service Unions* v. *Minister for the Civil Service* [1985] A.C. 374.
[6] [1986] Q.B. 556.
[7] [1983] 2 A.C. 629.
[8] [1972] 2 Q.B. 299.
[9] [1979] Q.B. 425.
[10] [1984] 1 W.L.R. 1337.
[11] [1976] 1 W.L.R. 1052.
[12] *Wheeler* v. *Leicester City Council* [1985] A.C. 1054.
[13] *The Times*, June 18, 1987.
[14] [1981] A.C. 75.
[15] [1985] A.C. 318.
[16] *R.* v. *Secretary of State for the Environment, Ex p. London Borough of Brent* [1982] Q.B. 593.
[17] *British Oxygen Corporation* v. *Minister of Technology* [1971] A.C. 610.

The Boundaries of Judicial Review

MICHAEL J. BELOFF Q.C.*

I. *Introduction*

Law reform in England can rarely, if ever, fight itself free of the fetters of the past. The editors of the Supreme Court Practice describe the innovations introduced by S.I. 1977 No. 1955 as creating "a uniform, flexible and comprehensive code of procedure for the exercise by the High Court of its supervisory jurisdiction over the proceedings and decisions of inferior Courts, Tribunals or other bodies of persons charged with the performance of public acts and duties."[1] But the new Order 53, now given statutory backing in sections 29 and 31 of the Supreme Court Act 1981, states that the prerogative orders will only be granted in cases where the Court had power to grant them "immediately before the commencement of (the) Act"[2]: and declarations, injunctions or damages will only be granted under the new procedure against persons or bodies susceptible to the prerogative orders themselves, if not necessarily only where prerogative relief would have been available in the alternative.[3] So one of the boundaries of judicial review is defined by the hallowed case law identifying the kind of body, and the types of action, in respect of which the historic supervisory jurisdiction of the Court by way of those orders can be called into play. This much might reasonably have been anticipated in a legal system whose development owes so great a debt to judge-made law and which has always treated the prerogative orders—formerly writs—as *sui generis*. Greater gifts of prophecy might have been required to predict that the judges themselves would not be satisfied with the new procedures furnished them by the Rules Committee and the Legislature. The House of Lords in the leading case of *O'Reilly* v. *Mackman*[4] determined that if proceedings are directed to challenging the decisions of a

---

* This article is based upon a paper delivered to the Administrative Law Workshop of the inaugural Bar Conference on May 27, 1986.

public authority, as a general rule an application for judicial review will be not, as previously, an option, but, henceforth, an obligation. So another of the boundaries of judicial review is defined by the post-1981 case law identifying the kind of circumstances in which the supervisory jurisdiction of the Court through this medium has to be called into play.

It should, at the outset, be noted, that the boundary walls of procedural exclusivity rest upon different foundations. "When a litigant is denied judicial review under Order 53 and forced to proceed by way of action this is done because his case falls outside Section 31(2). When, on the other hand, a litigant is forced to proceed by way of application for judicial review, this is done because the public policy of protecting public authorities, operating through the abuse of process jurisdiction, so determines."[5]

I wish in this article and against this background to examine these questions:

  (i)   When as a matter of procedure is judicial review not available?

 (ii)   When as a matter of procedure must judicial review be used?

(iii) Is the *status quo* satisfactory or not?

II. *When is Judicial Review not available?*

I was, at the time of delivery of the paper upon which this article is based, able to state with confidence that judicial review is clearly not available when redress is sought in respect of the activities of a domestic body or tribunal—even if their decisions have consequences affecting the public. This principle, well recognised in relation to the prerogative orders before the reforms of 1977 and 1981, was apparently shown to retain its force unimpaired in their wake by the decision of *Law* v. *National Greyhound Racing Board*[6] where it was held that the exercise of the stewards' authority to suspend a trainer's licence, derived as it was from contract, could be challenged only by private law procedure. It would, however, be unwise to assume that for this purpose the definitive distinction is between bodies established by statute, statutory instrument or the royal prerogative on the one hand, and those which are established by different means on the other. No less a scholar than Professor Sir William Wade Q.C. has expressed doubts as to whether the decisions of bodies such as the disciplinary committee of Lloyds or of the General Medical Council, "domestic" bodies which do derive their powers from legislative enactment, are properly judicially reviewable,[7] although an authority of arguably co-ordinate status, the Court of Appeal, has felt no such scruples: (*Gee* v. *General Medical Council*).[8] If statutory or analogous source is not, in the eyes of one academic, a sufficient criterion of reviewability, it now appears that, in the eyes of the Master of the Rolls, it is not a necessary one. In *R.* v. *Panel on Take-overs and Mergers, ex p. Datafin*[9] the Court of Appeal held that the decisions of the self-regulatory City Take-Over Panel were subject to review by the Court, and that, accordingly, its decisions could be quashed on the conventional grounds of irrationality or unfairness. The Court of Appeal found that the Panel performed a public duty in its regulation of the financial markets and that it would be unthinkable to allow it to be "cocooned" from the attention of the Courts. For reviewability under Order 53 "the only essential elements are what can be described as a public element, which may take many different forms and the exclusion from the jurisdiction of bodies whose sole source of power is a consensual submission to the jurisdiction."[10]

This conclusion, (strictly *obiter dictum* since the application was dismissed on its merits), represents the triumph of substance over form—the functions of the Panel are indeed no different from what they would be, were that body the creature of statute (as indeed it may be in the future, if the climate of opinion moves decisively against self-regulation for the City)—but it certainly surprised any public lawyer reared on the ancient orthodoxies. And by approaching the issue on the footing that the established criteria for the engagement of judicial review were normal rather than normative, the Court of Appeal may have promulgated a judgment as significant for the long-term forward march of judicial review as *R.* v. *Northumberland Compensation Appeal Tribunal, ex p. Shaw*[11] (resumption of quashing for error of law on the face of the record), *Ridge* v. *Baldwin*[12] (rediscovery of natural justice) or *Anisminic Ltd* v. *Foreign Compensation Commission*[13] (definition of the jurisdictional limits of inferior tribunals and administrative bodies). For who can now say with confidence where the outer limits of judicial review lie? The tide of judicial pragmatism is washing away the marks of fertile dissent left by Lord Denning on the beaches of the common law: but his analogy between the role in modern society of "domestic" bodies such as the Stock Exchange, the Jockey Club, the Football Association and major Trade Unions in *Breen* v. *A.E.U.*[14] repays study and may now point the way forward to new horizons. "(Such bodies) have" he

Handwritten margin notes: No! Lloyds '93 Case; Bub Aga Khan Case.; Admin function, not judicial.

said pertinently "quite as much power as statutory bodies . . . They can make or mar a man by their decisions. Not only by expelling him from membership, but also by refusing to admit him as a member: or, it may be, by a refusal to grant a licence or to give their approval."[15] Private such bodies may be in foundation, but they are public in function—and thus may well in future find themselves vulnerable to the public law remedies of judicial review.[16]

But new perspectives only add to old problems. The dividing line between public and private authorities is not clear cut even on pre-*Datafin* law. The point is proved by the wealth of case law on the Public Authorities Protection Act 1893 (repealed in 1954) which set a time limit of six months, later extended to a year, on actions against public authorities acting in execution or intended execution of any Act of Parliament.[17] It has, for example, still to be finally determined into which category colleges or universities fall (*ex p. Roffey*[18] *Herring* v. *Templeman*[19]). It seems that a related academic institution—the college or university visitor—is subject to judicial review (*Thomas* v. *University of Bradford*).[20] and yet is traditionally a product of private foundation—even if a modern university, created by royal charter, could be subsumed under the generic heading of an emanation of the prerogative.

In any event it is not only the nature of the body, but the nature of that body's activity which has to be considered when choice of form of proceedings has to be made. An employee of a public authority who complains about the fact or manner of his sacking must prima facie sue for breach of contract or make an application to an industrial tribunal for unfair dismissal, *vide ex p. Walsh*[21] where the Court of Appeal held that judicial review was not available to a senior nursing officer who complained that there had been a breach of natural justice in applying official procedures leading to his dismissal. It is otherwise if the procedures are statutory or the employee enjoys office or status such as a prison officer (*ex p. Benwell*[22]). This difference is simple to state, to apply more difficult.[23] For it has been powerfully argued that the *G.C.H.Q.* case,[24] in which the propriety of the selected judicial review procedure was never questioned by Courts or Counsel, was on true analysis concerned only with the private rights of employees to belong to a Trades Union.[25] It will not only be in the discrete field of employment that such a problem of classification will arise. Thus in *R.* v. *I.B.A. ex p. Rank*[26] it was held that the ban by I.B.A. on Rank exercising certain voting rights attendant on its ownership of shares in the Granada Group emanated from powers conferred by the Group's articles of association, and not from the

Broadcasting Act 1981. And in *R.* v. *N.C.B. ex p. N.U.M.*[27] it was held that a decision by the Coal Board to close Bates Colliery was an executive, business or management decision akin to one taken by a public company, and not part of its activities as a public body. In both cases a judge in the Crown Office list held an application for judicial review to be incompetent.[28]

Let me consider one further instance of topical importance and but recently the subject of any judicial pronouncement—contract compliance. Local authorities in the United Kingdom are increasingly seeking to use their commercial power to ensure that their contractors pursue, and are seen to be pursuing, particular policies, for example anti-discrimination or pro trade-union, or that such contractors maintain an embargo on any form of contact with South Africa. Suppose a disappointed contractor, disqualified from tendering for a particular job because of failure to sign some required and relevant undertaking, wished to challenge such disqualification as being a misuse of the local authority's powers to enter into contract, would this be a claim to be mounted by way of judicial review? Would the correct analysis be that the local authority's position was indistinguishable from that of a private person who would enjoy, absent some specific statutory bar, freedom of choice as to with whom he would contract? Or would the fact that it was a public body and that its powers had a statutory source, demand that its activity be classified as a public law one?[29]

As this example shows, at the outer boundaries of judicial review, the issue may be not simply what remedy, but whether a remedy at all, for, in particular in the area of refusal to enter into contractual relations, private bodies may enjoy immunities from legal challenge which their public equivalents do not enjoy.

As a broad proposition, however, one can assert that private bodies, even if exercising public functions, or public bodies, when exercising private functions, are outside the outer boundaries of judicial review. But problems of definition and classification make the outer boundary a perplexing perimeter.

III. *When must Judicial Review be used?*—Uhes

I turn from the outer to the inner boundaries of judicial review where the issue is not whether a remedy, but what remedy. In *O'Reilly* v. *Mackman*[30] Lord Diplock propounded the proposition that it would "as general rule be contrary to public policy, and as such an abuse of the process of the Court, to permit a person seeking to establish that a decision of a public authority infringed rights to which he was entitled under public law to proceed by way of ordinary action and by this means to evade the provisions of Order 53 for the protection of such authorities."[31] This general rule was not required by either Order 53 in its reformed guise, nor by the Supreme Court Act 1981. It flew in the face of the contrary recommendation of the Law Commission, whose report inspired the new procedures.[32]

The mischief which those procedures were designed to cure was the deficiencies of the unreformed law from the perspective of the applicant—the inability to claim declaratory or injunctive relief or damages in conjunction with or by way of alternative to the prerogative orders, the absence of facility for discovery, or cross-examination. They were not designed to eliminate any perceived oppression from the viewpoint of public authorities resulting from use of the writ action to challenge the *vires* of their acts or decisions. No suggestion had ever been made in—to name but a few cases—*Ridge* v. *Baldwin*,[33] *Laker Airways*,[34] *Congreve*[35] or *Gouriet*[36] that the respondents were embarrassed because the applicants had by use of such procedure obviated the need to obtain the leave which would have been required had they sought a prerogative order; indeed in the last of these cases Lord Diplock himself extolled the virtues of the declaration, sought by writ, in the public law sphere.[37]

The conferment of special privileges on public authorities in litigation had previously been a matter for the legislature: e.g. the Public Authorities Protection Act 1893 or the Crown Proceedings Act 1947 (although this statute also illustrated the trend towards the removal of such privileges). Yet on this occasion the judiciary rushed in where the legislature (and rules committee) had feared to tread; and their reasoning that Order 53 had "remove(d) all the disadvantages" which had previously existed was ill-founded. The requirement of leave, the restrictive limitation period, the absence of automatic entitlement to discovery, interrogatories, oral evidence or cross-examination all still distinguish judicial review from writ action: and make it, or are capable of making it, a less potent procedure than the latter.[38]

But whether the decision was right or wrong—and as Counsel for the unsuccessful party I must belatedly declare an interest—litigants and lawyers must learn to live with the law as laid down by the House of Lords. It is not a comfortable exercise. Two issues are brought into play; firstly the issue of whether the rights of the citizen which it is alleged are infringed are public or private law rights: secondly whether, even if they are public law rights, the general rule admits—as a general rule must—of an exception in the particular circumstances of the case. So the inner boundary, like the outer boundary of judicial review, is not a limit clearly drawn by the legislative or judicial cartographer: but requires exploration and argument before it can finally be determined.

The ambit of the general rule is linked, if not indissolubly, to the fashionable—and from a common law perspective—novel concept of "public law," which at least one Judge, Lord Justice Parker has recently described as enjoying "no particular merit."[39] In *Cocks* v. *Thanet*[40] a distinction was drawn (in the context of a claim against a local authority for the provision of housing accommodation for the applicant and his family under the Housing (Homeless Persons) Act 1977) between decision making functions, i.e. consideration of whether the applicant for housing satisfied the criteria of the Act, and the executive functions i.e. affording of housing to an applicant adjudged to satisfy such criteria. Performance of the former can be challenged, if at all, as a public law matter by way of judicial review; non-performance of the latter by way of action in respect of breach of statutory duty, although mandamus might be thought to be the obvious weapon for enforcement of an enacted duty. But if public law decisions spawn private rights and duties the line between public and private is slender indeed.

In *Davy* v. *Spelthorne*[41] where a litigant sued a public authority for the careless advice of its officers that he should not appeal against an enforcement notice with the result that he lost the chance of successfully so doing, it was held that a writ action was appropriate since his claim sounded in negligence. A public authority may accordingly be sued in tort, contract or—one may presume—in respect of the breach of other common law or equitable rights in the manner appropriate to a civil action.

But the difficulty of determining whether public or private law rights are in issue is further illustrated by the case of *Gillick* v. *D.H.S.S.*[42] where the House of Lords held that the department's guidance to doctors in respect of the provision of contraceptives to girls under the age of 16 was lawful. Mrs Gillick proceeded by way of writ action for a declaration. Two of the Law Lords considered that she was seeking to vindicate her private rights as a parent. (Lord Fraser at 163: Lord Scarman at 178); two that her claim was in public law (Lord Bridge at 192: Lord Templeman at 207); and the remaining member did not address the issue at all (Lord Brandon). Lord Templeman however observed

"In the present case the proceedings are not in form judicial review proceedings but at this stage the technicality can be ignored because the legal issues raised in these proceedings cannot be allowed to remain unanswered."

IV. Exceptions to the General Rule

What then are the exceptions to the general rule (other than, when, like Lord Templeman in *Gillick*, a Law Lord simply and pragmatically chooses to ignore it)?

Lord Diplock in *O'Reilly* v. *Mackman* identified two. Lord Diplock's first exception was "where the invalidity of the decision arises as a collateral issue in a claim for infringement of a right of the Plaintiffs arising under private law"[43]: for instance an action for damages for wrongful arrest where the *vires* of a statutory power to detain is put in issue; (a classic example is provided by *Cooper* v. *Wandsworth Board of Works*[44] when the plaintiff successfully sued for trespass to land when the defendants, acting under statutory powers, had caused his house to be demolished without giving him a hearing).

Lord Diplock here seems to be suggesting that if the public law issue is *merely* subsidiary or incidental to the private law claim then a writ action is apposite. In a subsequent case, however, *A.B.B.* v. *Milk Marketing Board*[45] Sir John Donaldson M.R. reached the same conclusion when, in his analysis, "the public and private law issues were not even collateral to one another. They are inextricably intertwined" i.e. the public law issue was *not* merely subsidiary.

Lord Diplock's second exception was "where none of the parties objects to the adoption of the procedure by writ or originating summons"[46]: although unless the prospective defendant or respondent waives such objection in advance it would be imprudent to rely on any good grace after the issue of proceedings. Lord Scarman identified *Gillick* as an example of both exceptions.[47]

A third exception was provided by the case of *Wandsworth London B.C.* v. *Winder*[48] where it was held that in an action by a local authority for possession of a council flat for non-payment of rent, the tenant was entitled to defend and counterclaim in the ordinary way, even though the substance of his defence (scarcely collateral!) was that the authority's decisions to increase the rent were ultra vires and void. Presumably had the tenant acted pre-emptively and sought to challenge the vires of the authority's decision *before* any additional rent was claimed against him the rule in *O'Reilly* v. *Mackman* would have been applied in its full rigour. But it has been shown in the civil (as in the criminal[49]) field to be a shield, not a sword. The House of Lords could not in *Winder* bring themselves to say that the animal was wicked—or in legal language acting abusively—because when he was attacked, he defended himself.

A fourth exception, noted by Lord Denning M.R. in the Court of Appeal in *O'Reilly* v. *Mackman*,[50] is where the sheer scale of the case (on account of the discovery involved) made it unsuitable for a procedure avowedly expeditious in its nature: see *Air Canada* v. *Secretary of State for Trade*[51] where a group of airlines sought, *inter alia,* declarations that the British Airport Authority had unlawfully increased landing charges at Heathrow Airport but which in fact never proceeded to a full hearing.

A fifth exception was identified by Lord Scarman in *R.* v. *I.R.C., ex p. Rossminster*[52] who stated "if issues of fact or law are raised, which it is neither just nor convenient to decide without full trial process, the Court may dismiss the application (for judicial review) or order, in effect a trial."[53] Likewise in *R.* v. *Jenner*[54] (criminal proceedings for alleged contravention of a stop order) Tasker Watkins L.J. said "The procedure of judicial review, which rarely allows the reception of oral evidence, is not suited to resolving the issues of fact involved in deciding whether activity said to be prohibited by it is caught by Section 90." There are, of course, despite the substantive limitations of judicial review, many cases where issues of fact may fall for determination before the questions of law can be decided. What procedures were in fact followed by a disciplinary tribunal in the public sector? (This was the very issue in *O'Reilly* v. *Mackman* when the prisoners alleged, *inter alia,* that the Chairman of the Board of Visitors had refused to allow them to call alibi witnesses). What considerations were in fact taken into account, or not taken into account, by a public authority? Was the immigrant an illegal entrant (and thus liable to removal) because he had entered the United Kingdom by deception or not?[55] But if the Scarman approach—which predated *O'Reilly* v. *Mackman*—retains its validity, then the exceptions may start to swallow up the rule.

A sixth exception was noted in *A.B.B.* v. *M.M.B.*[56] (action for damages for alleged breach by the M.M.B. of its duties under E.E.C. law) when Sir John Donaldson M.R. held that Order 53 was "wholly inappropriate for any non-discretionary claim."

A seventh exception is presumably the right of the Attorney-General to bring proceedings as guardian of the public interest: and the analogous right of a local authority to bring proceedings on behalf of the inhabitants of an area (Local Government Act 1972, s.222).[57] Lord Diplock in *O'Reilly* counselled a "case by case" approach.[58] likewise Lord Scarman in *Gillick*[59]: But this is—and has been shown to be—a receipt for uncertainty. The wealth of academic commentary on the theme of procedural exclusivity in public law,[60] expounding with apparent relish the perceived inconsistencies and irrationalities of judgments in post *O'Reilly* cases, suggests that, absent Lord Diplock's unique facility
for legal analysis, the inner boundaries of judicial review remain unclear and controversial. And the abnormal variety of approaches by the Courts—and the divisions of opinions in particular cases at particular levels among the judiciary underscore the conclusion.

It is instructive to consider whether a House of Lords chaired by Lord Wilberforce might not have reached a different decision in the *O'Reilly* case. In his memorial to Lord Diplock,[61] Lord Wilberforce noted the "rather exceptional factual situation" of *O'Reilly* v. *Mackman*; spoke of the "careful reservations" to Lord Diplock's generalisation "not always recognised by Courts or commentators": and mused on how far Lord Diplock "will have succeeded in making this public/private law dichotomy stick." In *Davy* v. *Spelthorne* he uttered this salutary warning

> "Before the expression 'public law' can be used to deny a subject a right of action in the Court of his choice, it must be related to a positive prescription of law, by statute or statutory rules. We have not yet reached the point at which the mere characterisation of a claim as a claim in public law is sufficient to exclude it from consideration by the ordinary courts: to permit this would be to create a dual system of law with the rigidity and procedural hardship for Plaintiffs which it was the purpose of recent reforms to remove."[62]

But is this not just what has been achieved?[63]

V. *Conclusion*

For my part I do not consider the present situation satisfactory.

The developing willingness of the Courts to act as watchdogs over the executive will be undermined if litigants find themselves enmeshed in a new web of procedural technicalities largely spun of different threads from the old. It is a reproach to a mature system of jurisprudence that procedural objections taken by astute public bodies can delay, or even prevent the citizen from enjoying, a hearing of the merits of his claim.[64] It is of note in this context that the quartet of cases, which refined the rule in *O'Reilly* v. *Mackman*, all went ultimately to the House of Lords: local authorities, funded by ratepayers' monies, had played the procedural game for all it was worth. It is a further reproach to such a system that the same set of factual circumstances, giving rise to a set of complaints that are in substance siblings, should involve the issue of separate sets of proceedings with dissimilar time scales, procedural machinery and remedies. In *Davy* v. *Spelthorne*[65] there was a composite claim with a triple cause of action: two (seeking to restrain the local authority from implementing the enforcement notice, and to set that notice aside) were struck out as being public law claims: one—the negligence action—alone survived. The curious conclusion of the House of Lords was that the complainant should correctly have issued proceedings for judicial review as well as a writ action.

Moreover, the litigant who finds himself inside the maze is not guaranteed an exit. The rules of the Supreme Court do not allow for conversion of a writ action into an application for judicial review; and if a writ action is struck out by reference to the *O'Reilly* v. *Mackman* principle a later application for judicial review will usually fall foul of the stringent time limits associated with Order 53.[66] (At one stage in the *Winder* case the tenant did seek to apply for leave to seek judicial review but was refused because he was out of time. Mercifully his success in the House of Lords rendered this failure harmless).[67] Nor will adoption of a principle of "safety first" by reliance on the provisions of RSC Ord. 53 r. 9 (5) which allow conversion of an application for judicial review into a writ action provide a certain solution. The unfortunate Mr Walsh was not allowed to take that exit for the Master of the Rolls held the provision to be an anti-technicality rule designed to preserve the position of an applicant for relief who "finds that the *basis* of that relief is private law rather than public law." It was not designed "to allow him to amend and to claim different relief."[68] Since Mr Walsh had not asked for a declaration that his dismissal was a nullity, he had to go back to square one. Whether he did so and what were the consequences the law reports do not relate.

There are three possible solutions to the problem posed by the rule in *O'Reilly* v. *Mackman* and its aftermath.

The first is to seek, in an appropriate case, to persuade the House of Lords to overrule itself and restore the *status quo ante*: i.e. litigants' option as to procedure. There is recent precedent for the House so swiftly to have second thoughts about an earlier decision: see *ex p. Khawaja*[69] when it overruled its decision in *Re Zamir*[70] as to the indicia of an illegal entrant under the Immigration Act 1971. However this was in the context of construction of a statute: similar flexibility could not reasonably be anticipated in the context of a manifestly judge-made rule about procedure.[71]

The second is to seek to assimilate public law procedure, as it applies both to prerogative orders and to private law remedies, more closely to private law procedure; leave would need to be sought in any form of proceedings against a public body; thereafter the form of procedure would depend upon whether there were public law issues and whether there were disputes as to fact. This proposal, described by its proponent as "a sort of half-way house"[72] is dependent upon a satisfactory definition of public body complicated, and is, in one sense, retrograde since at present leave' is not required for *any* action against a public authority, e.g.: simple claim for breach of contract.

The third and, in my view, the only way out of the impasse is to reform in its entirety and by means of statute the system of remedies of public law, and to associate them with the remedies of private law, under a single procedure applicable to both—the "Wade solution."[73]

The present powers of the Court to strike out at the threshold actions which are, *inter alia*, frivolous or vexatious or without discernible merit and to refuse discretionary relief for inter alia, delay or adverse impact on third parties may be thought sufficient to deter or destroy the captious claims: and the Courts already have powers to allow trial on affidavit or order expedited hearings. However to the extent that special safeguards are thought appropriate for public authorities, these could be built into the reformed system, as a result of legislative enactment. Constitutional issues *are* at stake: this is a matter for Parliament, not the judiciary.

The existence of a unitary procedure would have the additional advantage of lessening, if not eliminating the need to classify a particular office or institution as "public" as distinct from "private." Judicial review needs to concentrate on issues of substance, not form. It appears to be at a cross-roads. Three decades of development may be succeeded by a period—but for how long?—of consolidation, anticipated by Lord Justice Woolf in his inaugural address to the Administrative Law Bar Association (October 30, 1986). The reader of the entrails will note;

(1) *Notts C.C.* v. *Secretary of State for the Environment*[74] ("the rate-capping case") where Lord Scarman emphasised the significance of Parliamentary approval of executive actions as a ground for refusing judicial review.

(2) *Pulhofer* v. *Hillingdon B.C.*[75] where the House of Lords suggested that the decisions of housing authorities about who was or was not homeless were best left to the administrators.[76]

(3) *Ex p. Swati*[77] where the Court of Appeal held that a visitor refused entry to the United Kingdom should ordinarily be required to leave and appeal under the statutory scheme, and not stay and seek judicial review of the refusal.

(4) *Yuen Hung Kong*[78] (by way of analogy) where the Privy Council limited the scope for negligence actions against public authorities.

Yet there is no certainty about the direction that public law will take in the future. Lord Diplock's reformulation of the principles upon which judicial review is based in the *G.C.H.Q.* case,[79] illegality, irrationality and procedural impropriety may appear a somewhat concentrated summary: but he contemplated the possibility of further growth with specific reference to the doctrine of proportionality. Lord Scarman himself said in the rate-capping case that judicial review is "not fossilised."[80]

The *Datafin* decision itself, although it dealt with the nature of the body liable to judicial review as distinct from the principles upon which review was based, is not the product of a uniformly conservative judiciary.

Lord Diplock boasted with reason that the strengthening of administrative law was "the greatest achievement of the English Courts in my judicial lifetime:" but the achievement is imperilled if the dichotomy of procedures provide the citizen with a trap rather than a target.[81] Some lawyers may rejoice in a state of affairs which allows such scope for procedure disputes, but it is not in the interests of litigants. Procedural law should be the servant, not the master, of substantive law.

Notes

1 1987 ed. Vol. 1, p. 791.
2 Supreme Court Act 1981 ("S.C.A."), s.29(1).
3 S.C.A. s.31(1), (2), (4); Order 53 ("O. 53") r. 1. See discussion in Forsyth "Beyond *O'Reilly* v. *Mackman*. The foundations and nature of procedural exclusivity" (1986) C.L.J. 415. In *R.* v. *Secretary of State for the Environment, ex p. GLC, The Times*, December 30, 1985, Woolf J. held that the Court would grant a declaration in respect of public law issues where it was just and convenient to do so, but it was neither just nor convenient if there was an alternative remedy, and the jurisdiction would not be exercised unless there was a point of general public importance which needed to be resolved in the public interest.
4 [1983] 2 A.C. 237.
5 Forsyth: op. cit. pp. 425–426.
6 [1983] 1 W.L.R. 1302. For the earlier law see *ex p. Lain* [1967] 2 Q.B. 864.
7 (1983) 99 *L.O.R.* 170 commenting on, *inter alia, R.* v. *Committee of Lloyds, The Times*, January 12, 1983.
8 [1986] 1 W.L.R. 1247, *per* Lloyd L.J. at 1252. See also 1987, W.L.R. 564 (H.L.)
9 [1987] Q.B. 815. See Wade "New vistas of judicial review" (1987) 103 L.Q.R. 323–327; Beatson " 'Public' and 'private' in English administrative law" (1987) vol. 103 L.Q.R. 34; Kinsella "Judicial review—nature of powers exercised" (1987) 46 C.L.J. 200; Forsyth (1987) *Public Law* 356. Cane (1987) C.J.Q. 324.
10 *Ibid.* at 838. see also *Re Guinos, The Times*, March 30, 1988.
11 [1952] 1 K.B. 338.
12 [1964] A.C. 40.
13 [1969] 2 A.C. 647.
14 [1971] 2 Q.B. 175.
15 *Ibid.* at 190. Woolf L.J. has recommended that the law *should* take such a turning: "Public law: private law, why the divide? A personal view" (1986) *Public Law*, 220. at 224–225.
16 Does the *Datafin* exclusion of judicial review where submission to jurisdiction is based on contract apply where the aggrieved party is not in a contractual relationship with the offending body, e.g. a person refused admission to a trade union? See, as to a related problem, *Cowley* v. *Heatley, The Times*, July 24, 1986. See also *Finnigan* v. *New Zealand Rugby Football Union* (1985) 2 N.Z.L.R. 159: judicial review granted of a decision of the Union to send a representative team to South Africa: although the Union was a private and voluntary association it was in a position of major national importance.
17 *Halsbury's Laws*, 3rd ed., Vol. 30. para. 1318.
18 [1969] 2 Q.B. 538
19 [1973] 1 W.L.R. 569. See also *Law* v. *National Greyhound Racing Club Ltd.* [1983] 1 W.L.R. 1302, *per* Lawton L.J. at 1307.
20 [1987] 2 W.L.R. 677, H.L. See Bridge "The Jurisdiction of the University Visitor" (1970) 86 L.Q.R. 631, and *ex p. Vijayatunga* [1987] 3 All E.R. 204, at 212. Hadfield (1987) *Public Law* at 323, note 19.
21 [1985] 1 Q.B. 152.
22 [1985] 1 Q.B. 554. See also *Connors* v. *Strathclyde Regional Council* 1986 S.L.T. 530; and *ex p. Jones, The Times*, June 19, 1986.

[23] See Cripps "Dismissal, jurisdiction and judicial review" (1985) 44 C.L.J. 177.

[24] [1985] A.C. 374.

[25] Wade "Procedure and prerogative in public law" (1985) 101 L.Q.R. 150.

[26] *The Times*, March 14, 1986, Mann J.; and March 26, 1986 C.A. (unreported).

[27] *The Times*, March 8, 1986. And what of the BBC? For rival arguments see: Boyle "Political broadcasting, fairness and administrative law" 1986 *Public Law* 562, at 589–592.

[28] In the former case this was upheld by the Court of Appeal. Now see *ex p. Harriott, The Times*, October 27, 1987: Schiemann J. said (*obiter*) that the advice of an advisory committee of a hospital (without statutory basis or function) might be subject to judicial review if, for example, it advised on racial grounds that a woman should be refused I.V.F. This propounds a new test of public consequences as distinct from public functions or public source.

[29] See Turpin *Government Contracts*, 1972, chap. 9 for the exercise of such power by the organs of central government. See *Equal Opportunities Review*, vol. 10 for the (former) G.L.C.'s approach. See *R.* v. *Lewisham London Borough Council, ex p. Shell U.K. Ltd.* [1988] 1 All E.R. 938; 151 L.G.R. 664.

[30] [1983] 2 A.C. 237.

[31] *Ibid.* at 285.

[32] Cmnd. 6407 para. 35.

[33] [1964] A.C. 10.

[34] [1977] Q.B. 643.

[35] [1976] Q.B. 629.

[36] [1978] A.C. 435.

[37] *Ibid.* at 501.

[38] See generally Wade "Procedure and prerogative in public law" (1985) 101 L.Q.R. 180.

[39] *Bourgoin* v. *Secretary of State for Agriculture* [1986] Q.B. 714 at p. 788.

[40] [1983] 2 A.C. 286.

[41] [1984] A.C. 262.

[42] [1986] A.C. 112. In *Guevara* v. *Hounslow London Borough Council, The Times*, April 17, 1987, it was held that when a claim (here for negligence and breach of statutory duty under ss. 18 and 21 of the Child Care Act 1980 for alleged failure to provide a child with accommodation or adequately to supervise him for a period in July or August 1984 when the plaintiff was in the defendant's care) involved a substantial public law element, the proper procedure was judicial review, albeit private law rights were also established.

[43] [1983] 2 A.C. 237, at 285.

[44] [1863] 14 C.B.N.S. 180.

[45] [1984] C.M.L.R. 584.

[46] [1983] 2 A.C. 237, at 285.

[47] [1986] A.C. 112, at 178.

[48] [1985] A.C. 761. But see (1988) 1 All E.R. 841.

[49] *R.* v. *Jenner* [1983] 1 W.L.R. 873. But now see *Quietlynn Ltd.* v. *Plymouth City Council* [1988] Q.B. 114. where it was held that, except in the case of a decision which was invalid on its face, criminal courts were bound when adjudicating in criminal proceedings for the statutory offence of using premises as sex establishments without a licence, to presume that the decisions of licensing authorities had been validly made unless struck down by the High Court in judicial review proceedings. But see *ex. p.* Hutchinson 1988 1 All E.R. 333.

[50] [1983] 2 A.C. 237, at 258–259.

[51] Reported on the issue of public interest privilege at [1983] 2 A.C. 394.

[52] [1980] A.C. 952.

[53] at 1028.

[54] [1983] 1 W.L.R. 873.

[55] *ex p. Khawaja and Khera* [1983] 2 A.C. 74.

[56] [1984] 2 C.M.L.R. 584.

[57] Lydiard, 5 *Litigation*, 1977.

[58] [1983] 2 A.C. 237, at 285.

[59] [1986] A.C. 112, at 178.

[60] Much of the literature is referred to by Forsyth at 1986 C.L.J. 415.

[61] (1985) *Public Law* 6–7.

[62] [1984] 1 A.C. 262, at 276.

[63] For a powerful defence of the rule in *O'Reilly* v. *Mackman* see Woolf L.J. op. cit. at pp. 231–234.

[64] For an empirical study see Sunkin "What is happening to applications for judicial review?" 1987 *M.L.R.* 432.

[65] [1984] A.C. 262. For an instance of a failure by a local authority to succeed on a technical point see *Ettridge* v. *Morrell* (1986) 85 L.G.R. 100, C.A., where a National Front candidate resisted an attempt by the ILEA to strike out his action for a declaration that he was entitled under the Representation of the People Act 1985 to have a suitable room made available to him. The Court held that he had a private law right and was not obliged to proceed by way of application for judicial review.

[66] S.C.A. 1981, s.31(6), Order 53, r. 4. *ex p. Jackson* [1985] 1 W.L.R. 1319.

[67] Woolf L.J. writes " . . . If there comes before the High Court a case which has obvious merit, the Court can then and there give leave and treat the material which is before it as fulfilling the procedural requirements of an application for judicial review, and this is what I have done on more than one occasion" (op. cit. at 232). Citizens' rights should not depend upon the clemency of individual judges!

[68] [1985] 1 Q.B. 152, at 166. Now see *ex p. Dew* ([1987] 1 W.L.R. 881) where McNeill J. held that where the relief sought on an application for judicial review was a declaration, an injunction or damages the Court's discretionary power under R.S.C. Order 53, r. 9(5) to order the proceedings to continue as if begun by writ was only exercisable if the alleged breach of a public law obligation had, as a consequence, an entitlement to damages in private law, and, if an application for judicial review was struck out as disclosing no arguable complaint in public law the Court could not make an order under r. 9(5) that the proceedings continue as if begun by writ. On the facts the prisoner/applicant's cause of action involved no arguable complaint in public law but was a private law action for damages for negligence in failing to provide proper medical treatment and had been such from the commencement. Accordingly it was a misuse of procedure to seek relief by way of judicial review and the application would be struck out with the result that no order could be made under r. 9(5) in the applicant's favour. This all but closes the escape route of Order 59 r. 9(5). For use of that route, however, see *ex p. Phillips, The Times,* November 21, 1986.

[69] [1983] 2 A.C. 74.

[70] [1980] A.C. 930.

[71] An attempt was made in *Wandsworth* v. *Winder* ([1985] 1 A.C. 461, at 497) but not even alluded to in the speeches.

[72] Cane, *Administrative Law* p. 179

[73] (1985) 101 L.Q.R. 180.

[74] [1986] A.C. 240.

[75] [1986] A.C. 484.
[76] See Lord Brightman at 518.
[77] [1986] 1 W.L.R. 477.
[78] [1988] A.C. 145. see also 1988 2 W.L.R. 418.
[79] *Council of Civil Service Unions* v. *Minister for the Civil Service* [1986] A.C. 374, at 410H.
[80] [1986] A.C. 249.
[81] See generally Sir Patrick Neill Q.C. "Administrative Law Ladders and Snakes" Child Co. lecture 1985, pp. 28–32.

What is a Public Authority for the Purposes of Judicial Review?

DAVID PANNICK

I. *Introduction*

"I know of no duty of the Court which it is more important to observe, and no power of the Court which it is more important to enforce," said Lindley M.R. in 1899, "than its power of keeping public bodies within their rights. The moment public bodies exceed their rights they do so to the injury and oppres-sion of private individuals, and those persons are entitled to be protected from injury arising from such operations of public bodies."[1]

Notwithstanding the importance of this jurisdiction of the courts, until the 1970's it was rare for public bodies to have their decisions declared unlawful by the courts. This was, I suspect, less because public bodies always understood and applied the law of the land, more because litigation was, in those far-off days, not seen as the common response to an unfavourable determination of a public authority.

The novel pressures imposed on government by the developing doctrines of administrative law came to a head in 1975. The Court of Appeal held unlawful the Home Secretary's plan to revoke television licences taken out to avoid a forthcoming increase in the licence fee. Lord Denning reprimanded counsel for the Home Secretary for submitting that "if the court interferes in this case, 'it would not be long before the powers of the court would be called in question'."[2]

Counsel's submission in that case was the last, desperate cry of a dying order. Liberating reforms to the Rules of the Supreme Court in 1977 and later improvements in the procedure for hearing applications for judicial review[3] swept away the obscure technicalities which had previously fettered judicial review of administrative action. "The curtains were drawn back. The light was let in."[4] In consequence, court "interference" in the decisions of public bodies is now taken for granted.

In the last ten years, there has been an enormous growth in the business of the Divisional Court. The number of applications for judicial review has more than doubled since 1981.[5] The caseload involves high profile issues at the intersections of law and politics as well as habitual challenges to individual decisions made by an ever-growing army of bureaucrats. In the last two or three years, an increasing number of large public companies have begun to realise that judicial review is not the exclusive concern of civil liberties lawyers and their clients and that the use (or the threat) of the weapon of judicial review can achieve positive results in the commercial sphere.

It is easy to see why the Divisional Court is so popular. Cases can be brought on very speedily. Because the evidence is by affidavit, with cross-examination extremely rare, the hearings do not occupy much court time. The need to obtain leave before commencing judicial review proceedings enables the client to obtain, at low cost, the opinion of a High Court judge on whether the case is arguable. The judges who sit in the Divisional Court are experts who know and understand the law.

The Divisional Court performs the most important and sensitive function in English law: it holds the balance of power between the individual and government (local and central). Unfortunately, the rapid development of administrative law has allowed little time for the courts to consider the principles on which judicial review is granted. In particular, it remains unclear what is a "public body" and when its decisions are amenable to judicial review. The statute and the Rules of the Supreme Court which govern an application for judicial review provide no guidance on what is a public body for the purposes of an application for the remedies of certiorari, mandamus and prohibition (which can be, and now are, claimed in conjunction with a declaration and an injunction). Section 31 of the Supreme Court Act 1981 and Order 53 of the Rules of the Supreme Court say nothing about the bodies in respect of whose decisions such an application can be made except to indicate, unhelpfully, that one of the matters to which the High Court should have regard in deciding whether to grant a declaration or an injunction in such proceedings is "the nature of the persons and bodies against whom relief may be granted by such orders."[6] As in so many aspects of judicial review of administrative action, the relevant principles of law have to be extracted from judicial decisions.

It is clear that "as a result of a series of judicial decisions since about 1950... there has been a dramatic and indeed a radical change in the scope of judicial review."[7] The prerogative writs were once confined to the acts or omissions of inferior courts and tribunals. They now control the conduct of a wide range of public bodies.

The starting point for modern judicial consideration of the scope of judicial review is the decision of Lord Justice Atkin in *R. v. Electricity Commissioners, ex p. London Electricity Joint Committee Company (1920) Ltd.* Atkin L.J. (with the agreement of Younger L.J.) stated that,

> "[w]herever any body of persons having legal authority to determine questions affecting the rights of subjects, and having the duty to act judicially, act in excess of their legal authority they are subject to the controlling jurisdiction of the King's Bench Division ... ".[8]

The third judge, Bankes L.J., confined himself to saying that a prerogative order will lie against "a body exercising judicial functions . . . ."[9]

In 1967, in *R. v. Criminal Injuries Compensation Board, ex p. Lain*, Lord Parker C.J. said that Lord Justice Atkin's judgment was not "intended to be an exhaustive definition" of the scope of the supervisory jurisdiction of the courts. That scope is broad enough to cover bodies exercising prerogative, as opposed to statutory, powers. Furthermore, Atkin L.J. had not

> "intended to confine his principle to cases in which the determination affected rights in the sense of enforceable rights ... [T]he remedy is available even though the decision is merely a step as a result of which legally enforceable rights may be affected."

Lord Parker suggested that

> "the exact limits of the ancient remedy by way of certiorari have never been and ought not to be specifically defined. They have varied from time to time being extended to meet changing conditions... We have ... reached the position when the ambit of certiorari can be said to cover every case in which a body of persons of a public as opposed to a purely private or domestic character has to determine matters

affecting subjects provided always that it has a duty to act judicially."[10]

The next major case to consider the ambit of judicial review was *O'Reilly* v. *Mackman*. Lord Diplock said that he would broaden Lord Justice Atkin's description to remove the phrase "having the duty to act judicially." He suggested that judicial review would cover

> "a determination of a statutory tribunal or any other body of persons having legal authority to determine questions affecting the common law or statutory rights or obligations of other persons as individuals."[11]

In *C.C.S.U.* v. *Minister for the Civil Service* ("the G.C.H.Q. case"), the House of Lords confirmed that judicial review extends to the exercise of prerogative powers. Lord Diplock stated some broad principles:

> "[t]o qualify as a subject for judicial review the decision must have consequences which affect some person (or body of persons) other than the decision-maker, although it may affect him too. It must affect such other person either:
> (a) by altering rights or obligations of that person which are enforceable by or against him in private law; or
> (b) by depriving him of some benefit or advantage which either
>
> > (i) he had in the past been permitted by the decision-maker to enjoy and which he can legitimately expect to be permitted to continue to do until there has been communicated to him some rational grounds for withdrawing it on which he has been given an opportunity to comment; or
> > (ii) he has received assurance from the decision-maker will not be withdrawn without giving him first an opportunity of advancing reasons for contending that they should not be withdrawn . . .

For a decision to be susceptible to judicial review the decision-maker must be empowered by public law (and not merely, as in arbitration, by agreement between private parties) to make decisions that, if validly made, will lead to administrative action or abstention from action by an authority endowed by law with executive powers, which have one or other of the consequences mentioned [above]."[12]

What these, and other, judgments are working towards is a principle that a decision is subject to judicial review if two conditions are satisfied. First, the decision must be made by a public body, that is a person or institution empowered by statute, statutory instrument or prerogative powers or by other means (for example a Royal Charter or, perhaps, mere custom and practice) to perform public functions. Secondly, the decision complained of must be made by the relevant body in its public law capacity, that is so as to affect the public law rights, obligations or expectations of the victim. Each of these limbs continues to be productive of much uncertainty.

II. *Organisations subject to Judicial Review*

Although "in recent years the courts have not been slow to push the boundaries of the prerogative jurisdiction ever wider,"[13] there remained until very recently a basic condition to be satisfied before judicial review could be claimed. The court only enjoyed the judicial review powers in respect of a body whose functions derive from statute, statutory instrument or the exercise of the prerogative. A body whose powers derive from the agreement of the parties was, it was thought by public lawyers, not such a public body. Hence, "[p]rivate or domestic tribunals have always been outside the scope of certiorari since their authority is derived solely from contract...."[14] Section 31(2) of the Supreme Court Act 1981 has not expanded the nature of the bodies subject to judicial review and therefore the decisions of the disciplinary tribunal of the National Greyhound Racing Club are not judicially reviewable.[15] For the same reason a prerogative writ will not lie against an arbitrator acting pursuant to the agreement of the parties.[16]

These principles are not always easy to apply. Is an institution created by Royal Charter a public body for the purposes of judicial review?[17] In *R.* v. *Broadcasting Complaints Commission, ex p. Owen*, the Divisional Court expressly left open the difficult question of whether the BBC is subject to judicial review.[18] The BBC carries out important public functions and it would be odd if its performance of its powers and duties was not subject to the supervision of the Divisional Court. However, Parliament has chosen not to impose on the BBC the statutory framework pursuant to which the Independent Broadcasting Authority functions.

On at least one occasion[19] it has been assumed that certiorari could be claimed in respect of the decision of a University Senate to exclude a student from continuing his studies. This has been doubted by the Court of Appeal in a later case,[20] though less-on the ground that a University established by a Royal Charter is not a public body, more on the ground that a disciplinary decision is not within the realm of public law since it is made pursuant to a contract.[21] The Civil Service Appeal Board (which was created partly by the exercise of prerogative powers and partly by an agreement between management and trade unions in order to hear appeals by civil servants threatened with dismissal) is a public body whose decisions are subject to judicial review.[22]

The "growth of central and local government intervention in the affairs of the ordinary citizen since the Second World War and the consequent increase in the number of administrative bodies charged by Parliament with the performance of public duties"[23] has given the Divisional Court jurisdiction over an ever-expanding number of public bodies.

The public corporation is now put to so many uses that, as Professor Wade has explained, it "has no regular form and no specialised function." Newly created government departments, Regional Health Authorities, the Civil Aviation Authority and the public corporations which serve as "vehicles for the government's involvement in industry" have little in common, except the fact that they perform duties on behalf of the State.[24]

It is evident that "[t]he 'night-watchman' State is rapidly being replaced by a State whose functions range from welfare to commercial activities and from law and order to education," using a bewildering variety of bodies which carry out functions which are

> "allocated in a haphazard fashion. Some, like the Post Office, are transmogrified from departments of State to autonomous bodies overnight, yet carry out the same task and retain the same privileges. No activity is typically governmental in character nor wholly without parallels in private law. Even the most characteristic function may be delegated—as when the law and order function is exercised by private armies levied by Securicor, a private service employed on occasion by government agencies."[25]

There have been attempts, in various contexts to analyse the criteria of a public body for the purposes of English law. Relying on decisions in the context of now-repealed limitation provisions, *Halsbury's Laws* defines a "public authority" as "a person or administrative body entrusted with functions to perform for the benefit of the public and not for private profit."[26] Section 7 of the Public Bodies Corrupt Practices Act 1889 defines a "public body" by reference to the enjoyment of powers to act under and for the purposes of a statute.[27] Section 75(5) of the Race Relations Act 1976 defines "public body" to mean "a body of persons, whether corporate or unincorporate, carrying on a service or undertaking of a public nature." The decision of the European Court of Justice that provisions of the Equal Treatment Directive have direct effect only against State authorities[28] has led to a number of cases considering whether various bodies (from Rolls-Royce plc to the University of Glasgow) satisfy this test.[29]

Also of some assistance in attempting to identify what is a public body for the purposes of judicial review are the various cases where Courts have had occasion to consider the scope of Crown immunities. Rates do not have to be paid on property "occupied for the purposes of the government of the country...."[30] A house owned by the British Transport Commission (a statutory corporation over which the Minister of Transport had been given powers by Parliament) did not enjoy Crown immunity from the Rent Restriction Acts. Denning L.J., giving judgment for the Court of Appeal, said that the Commission "is, of course, a public authority and its purposes, no doubt, are public purposes, but it is not a government department nor do its powers fall within the province of government."[31] The BBC is not entitled to Crown immunity from taxation: broadcasting services are provided by an independent agency and not as a function of government.[32] However, the supply of a drug to National Health Service hospitals for administration to patients was a use "for the services of the Crown" (and so was exempted from the usual provisions of patent law).[33] Of course, all of these cases have to be considered in the light of their very different contexts.

The Divisional Court ought to construe its jurisdiction in the widest possible way. It exists to supervise the acts and omissions of all bodies or persons acting on behalf of the State, central or local, administrative or commercial. The question for the Court is whether the relevant body has been authorised by the State to perform public functions, that is the carrying out of duties and the exercise of powers on behalf of the public, in the interests of the community. The source of those powers and duties, whether statutory, prerogative, charter or other, is irrelevant in this context.

In the light of the growing strength of judicial review as an important means of protection of the rights of citizens against those who govern us, it is necessary to ask the question posed by Sir Harry Woolf (one of the most experienced judges in the field of administrative law): should judicial review be limited to public bodies? As he explained,

> "The interests of the public are as capable of being adversely affected by the decisions of large corporations and large associations, be they of employers or employees, and should they not be subject to challenge on *Wednesbury* grounds if their decision relates to activities which can damage the public interest? . . . Powerful bodies, whether they are public bodies or not, because of their economic muscle may be in a position to take decisions which at the present time are not subject to scrutiny and which could be unfair or adversely affect the public interest."[34]

Where a person has a contract with a private body not hitherto subject to judicial review (such as a trade union or a domestic tribunal), the courts have jurisdiction to hear a complaint from that individual that the body has incorrectly interpreted or applied its own rules to his detriment.[35] However, until recently it was thought that English law provides only limited protection for victims of the decisions of important (but private) bodies with whom they have no contractual relationship. Such bodies, it was believed, would find their decisions subject to the control of the court if they are in unreasonable restraint of trade (which appears to be treated as a tort in this context), or unreasonably interfere with the right to work, or apply a procedure in conflict with natural justice.[36] But the Court will

> "be slow to allow any implied obligation to be fair to be used as a means of bringing before the courts for review honest decisions of bodies exercising jurisdiction over sporting and other activities which those bodies are far better fitted to judge than the courts."[37]

Moreover, it was thought, the court has no jurisdiction to determine whether a trade union or a club, or other analogous body, has, in reaching an important decision, taken an irrelevancy into account or ignored relevant factors.[38] For similar reasons, it was held in 1825 that mandamus would not lie to compel the Benchers of Lincoln's Inn to admit a person as a member "even if they act capriciously upon the subject . . . ."[39] This was because "as far as the admission of members is concerned, these are voluntary societies, not submitting to any government. They may in their discretion admit or not as they please, and this court has no power to compel them to admit any individual."[40]

There are clear signs that the common law is rapidly developing in this respect. In 1985, the New Zealand Court of Appeal considered whether members of a local rugby club could challenge the decision of the New Zealand Rugby Football Union to send a national team to tour South Africa. The national body was not a public body but a private association. The aggrieved individuals were not members of the national body and had no contract with it. Nevertheless, its decision was a matter of considerable public importance. Mr Justice Cooke held, on behalf of the New Zealand Court of Appeal, that

> "In cases where an incorporated association is alleged to have acted against its objects but the plaintiff cannot show a contract, we think that all the circumstances of the case have to be considered—case by case or category of case by category of case—in order to determine as a question of mixed law and fact whether or not he or she has sufficient standing."

The court noted that the decision of the national body "affects the New Zealand community as a whole" and "the international relations or standing of New Zealand." Furthermore, the court noted,

> "While technically a private and voluntary sporting association, the Rugby Union is in relation to this decision in a position of major national importance . . . In truth the case has some analogy with public law issues. This is not to be pressed too far. We are not holding that, nor even discussing whether, the decision is the exercise of a statutory power . . . We are saying simply that it falls into a special area where, in the New Zealand context, a sharp boundary between public and private law cannot realistically be drawn."

The Court held that the plaintiffs had standing: they were members of the local clubs and so were linked to the Rugby Football Union by a chain of contracts.[41]

Despite the reluctance of the court to deal with the issue as one of jurisdiction, and its unpersuasive preference for tackling the problem as one of standing, the New Zealand case is important in indicating a move towards the broadening of the scope of judicial review. The national importance of the decision-making body and of the relevant decision may be factors which lead to judicial review of a decision of a private body even where the plaintiff has no contractual entitlement.

A similar process of reasoning was adopted by the Court of Appeal in *R.* v. *Panel on Take-Overs and Mergers, ex p. Datafin plc.* The court there rejected the complaint that the City's Take-overs Panel had misdirected itself in its policing of a take-over bid for the McCorquodale printing group. But, the court concluded, although the Panel is a regulatory body with no statutory or prerogative or common law powers, and although it was not in a contractual relationship with the financial market or those who dealt in that market, it is nevertheless subject to judicial review.

Sir John Donaldson M.R. explained that, in practice, the Panel's decisions have a substantial and binding impact on all those who want to do business in the City. Despite the fact that it appeared to be "without visible means of legal support," it "operates wholly in the public domain . . . performing a public duty and an important one . . . The rights of citizens are indirectly affected by its decisions . . . ." The Court would "recognise the realities of executive power" and would not be inhibited "by the subtlety and sometimes complexity of the way in which it can be exerted."[42]

For judicial review to stop short of such a powerful body would be unjustifiable. In the light of the impact of the Panel's decisions on business in the City, why should the acts and omissions of the Panel be immune from judicial supervision to ensure natural justice and the other basic requirements of fairness and good administration?

The significance of the Court of Appeal's decision is the recognition that, in some contexts, the private and "voluntary" sector governs Britain and that the functions of a body, and not merely its origin, may justify the application of the supervisory jurisdiction of the Divisional Court. Future cases will determine what other private bodies are subject to judicial review because of the significant functions they perform. Trade associations and sports' governing bodies now look vulnerable. The Court of Appeal has opened a new era in administrative law. The court has given administrative lawyers a much needed licence to conduct our own insider trading within important, but hitherto sacrosanct, private bodies.

III. *Private activities immune from review*

"Like public figures, at least in theory, public bodies are entitled to have a private life."[43] Not every decision of a public body is reviewable in the Divisional Court. Judicial review "is confined to reviewing activities of a public nature as opposed to those of a purely private or domestic character."[44] It is far from easy to determine how this principle will be applied to the facts of any particular case.

Judicial review will often not be available in relation to an employment decision of a public authority. The issue is whether the public body is exercising "an authority which affects the applicant's rights *qua* subject [or] the applicant's rights *qua* ... employee."[45] In *R.* v. *East Berkshire Health Authority, ex p. Walsh*, the Court of Appeal held that a senior nursing officer dismissed for alleged misconduct could not challenge the decision by way of judicial review. The court said that the criterion of judicial review was whether there was any "statutory underpinning" of the applicant's relationship with the respondent authority or whether, by contrast, it was a pure employer and employee relationship.[46] In *R.* v. *Secretary of State for the Home Department, ex p. Benwell*, Hodgson J. distinguished *Walsh* and held that a decision under the Code of Discipline for prison officers could be challenged by way of judicial review (because the Code was made by the Secretary of State pursuant to his powers under the Prison Rules 1964).[47] Other employment cases have reached varying conclusions on whether specific employment issues are susceptible to judicial review.[48]

Commercial decisions by public bodies may be immune from judicial review. In *R.* v. *National Coal Board, ex p. National Union of Mineworkers,* Mr Justice Macpherson held that the decision of the N.C.B. to close a colliery was an executive or business decision, similar to one taken by a public company, and so was not open to challenge in the Divisional Court.[49]

There are many prerogative powers the exercise of which could not be challenged by judicial review. In the G.C.H.Q. case, Lord Roskill stated that

"[p]rerogative powers such as those relating to the making of treaties, the defence of the realm, the prerogative of mercy, the grant of honours, the dissolution of Parliament and the appointment of ministers as well as others are not, I think, susceptible to judicial review because their nature and subject matter are such as not to be amenable to the judicial process. The courts are not the place wherein to determine whether a treaty should be concluded or the armed forces disposed in a particular manner or Parliament dissolved on one date rather than another."[50]

In these, and other circumstances, the courts may refuse to involve themselves in judicial review of the decisions of a public body.

IV. *Conclusion*

It is not surprising that, so soon after the birth of the modern principles of judicial review of administrative action, there remains considerable uncertainty about the directions in which, and how far along the route, this powerful and important doctrine will travel. What are "the needs of public administration" to which the courts will have regard?[51] In determining the substantive principles of judicial review, will the courts supplement the concept of *Wednesbury* unreasonableness,[52] and move towards a theory based on proportionality[53] and on fundamental human rights?[54] The next ten years of administrative law will be interesting for lawyers, governors and the governed.

Notes

[1] *Roberts* v. *Gwyrfai District Council* [1899] 2 Ch. 608, 614–615.
[2] *Congreve* v. *Home Office* [1976] Q.B. 629 at 652–653
[3] See Louis Blom-Cooper Q.C. "The New Face of Judicial Review: Administrative Changes in Order 53" 1982 *Public Law* 250.
[4] *O'Reilly* v. *Mackman* [1983] 2 A.C. 237 at 253 (Lord Denning in the Court of Appeal).
[5] See The Rt. Hon. Sir Harry Woolf "Public Law—Private Law: Why the Divide? A Personal View" 1986 *Public Law* 220 at 222.
[6] Section 31(2)(*b*) of the Supreme Court Act 1981 and Order 53, Rule 1(2)(*b*) of the Rules of the Supreme Court.
[7] *C.C.S.U.* v. *Minister for the Civil Service* [1985] A.C. 374 at 414 (Lord Roskill).
[8] [1924] 1 K.B. 171 at 205.
[9] *Ibid.* at 194.
[10] [1967] 2 Q.B. 864 at 881–882.
[11] Above note 4 at 279.

[12] Above note 7 at 408–409.
[13] *R.* v. *Post Office, ex p. Byrne* [1975] I.C.R. 221 at 224 (Bridge J. for the Divisional Court).
[14] *R.* v. *Criminal Injuries Compensation Board, ex p. Lain* above note 10 at 882.
[15] *Law* v. *National Greyhound Racing Club Ltd.* [1983] 1 W.L.R. 1302 (Court of Appeal). *Cf. O'Reilly* above note 4 at 256 where Lord Denning in the Court of Appeal suggested that section 31(2) is responsible for "expanding the kind of bodies against whom relief can be obtained."
[16] *R.* v. *National Joint Council for the Craft of Dental Technicians (Disputes Committee), ex p. Neate* [1953] 1 Q.B. 704.
[17] In *Pharmaceutical Society of Great Britain* v. *Dickson* [1970] A.C. 403—which was not a case of judicial review—Lord Upjohn said at page 434 that "the appellant society, being the creation of a Royal Charter, is not bound by the doctrines of ultra vires in the same way as a corporation created by or pursuant to a statute. A chartered corporation is not, as a matter of vires, bound by its Charter. At common law it has all the powers of an individual and can legally and lawfully extend its activities beyond the objects of its Charter and indeed carry out activities prohibited by the Charter. But its members, and only its members, can complain for if the corporation goes outside its expressed objects or, worse still, performs acts prohibited by the terms of the Charter, the Crown may by *scire facias* proceed to forfeit the Charter; any member can, therefore, apply to the court to prohibit the corporation from risking such forfeiture by continuing such activities."
[18] [1985] Q.B. 1153, 1172–1173.
[19] *R.* v. *Aston University Senate, ex p. Roffey* [1969] 2 Q.B. 538.
[20] *Herring* v. *Templeman* [1973] 3 All E.R. 569, 585, approved in *Law* above note 15 at 1307 *per* Lawton L.J. But *cf. O'Reilly* above note 4 at 256 where Lord Denning, in the Court of Appeal, cited *Roffey* with aproval.
[21] See part III below for a discussion of the principle that judicial review does not lie in respect of private law decisions of public bodies.
[22] *R.* v. *Civil Service Appeal Board, ex p. Bruce, The Times,* June 22, 1987 (Divisional Court).
[23] *R.* v. *I.R.C. ex p. National Federation of Self-Employed and Small Businesses Ltd.* [1982] A.C. 617 at 656 (Lord Roskill).
[24] H.W.R. Wade *Administrative Law* (5th edition: 1982), 139–142.
[25] Carol Harlow " 'Public' and 'Private' Law: Definition without Distinction" (1980) 43 *Modern Law Review* 241 at 257.
[26] *Halsbury's Laws of England* (4th edition), vol. 1, para. 6.
[27] A "public body" is there defined to mean "any council of a county or county of a city or town, any council of a municipal borough, also any board, commissioners, select vestry, or other body which has power to act under and for the purposes of any Act relating to local government, or the public health, or to poor law or otherwise to administer money raised by rates in pursuance of any public general Act . . . ". Section 4(2) of the Prevention of Corruption Act 1916 added to this the further category of "local and public authorities of all descriptions." See, on the interpretation of these provisions, *D.P.P.* v. *Holly* [1978] A.C. 43 where the House of Lords held that the North Thames Gas Board was a "public body" for this purpose.
[28] *Marshall* v. *Southampton and South West Hampshire Area Health Authority (Teaching)* [1986] Q.B. 401.
[29] See 319 *Industrial Relations Legal Information Bulletin* 12 (December 16, 1986). See also *Longden* v. *Bedfordshire County Council* (December 15, 1986: Peter Gibson J.—a Local Education Authority is not a State authority for this purpose) and *Rolls-Royce plc* v. *Doughty* [1981] I.C.R. 932 (E.A.T.).

[30] *Mersey Docks & Harbour Board Trustees* v. *Cameron* (1865) 11 H.L.C. 443 at 464.

[31] *Tamlin* v. *Hannaford* [1950] 1 K.B. 18 at 24.

[32] *BBC* v. *Johns* [1965] 1 Ch. 32 (Court of Appeal).

[33] *Pfizer Corporation* v. *Ministry of Health* [1965] A.C. 512 (House of Lords). See also *Nottingham No. 1 Area Hospital Management Committee* v. *Owen* [1958] 1 Q.B. 50, where the Divisional Court held that National Health Service hospitals were "premises occupied for the public service of the Crown" for the purposes of the Public Health Act 1936.

[34] Above note 5 at 224–225.

[35] *Lee* v. *The Showmen's Guild of Great Britain* [1952] 2 Q.B. 329 (Court of Appeal).

[36] See, for example, *Nagle* v. *Feilden* [1966] 2 Q.B. 633 (Court of Appeal) and *Enderby Town Football Club Ltd* v. *Football Association Ltd.* [1971] Ch. 591 at 606–7 (Lord Denning, with whom Cairns L.J. agreed).

[37] *McInnes* v. *Onslow-Fane* [1978] 1 W.L.R. 1520 at 1535 (Megarry V.–C.). See similarly *Cowley* v. *Heatley*, *The Times*, July 24, 1986 (Browne-Wilkinson V–C).

[38] *Hamlet* v. *GMBATU* [1987] 1 W.L.R. 449 at 452–453 (Harman J.).

[39] *R.* v. *The Benchers of Lincoln's Inn* (1825) 4 B. & C. 855 at 859–60 (Bayley J.).

[40] *Ibid.* at 861 *per* Littledale J.

[41] *Finnigan* v. *New Zealand Rugby Football Union Inc.* [1985] 2 N.Z.L.R. 159 at 178–80. See also *Finnigan (No. 3)* [1985] 2 N.Z.L.R. 190, where the Court of Appeal refused leave to appeal to the Judicial Committee of the Privy Council on this point of standing as it was, by that time, moot.

[42] [1987] 2 W.L.R. 699 at 711–15.

[43] Sir Harry Woolf above note 5 at 223.

[44] *R.* v. *B.B.C. ex p. Lavelle* [1983] I.C.R. 99 at 107 (Woolf J.).

[45] Above note 13 at 227.

[46] [1984] I.C.R. 743.

[47] [1984] I.C.R. 723.

[48] See, for example, *R.* v. *Hertfordshire County Council, ex p. NUPE* [1985] I.R.L.R. 258 (where the Court of Appeal heard, and dismissed on the merits, an application for judicial review of a decision to dismiss a number of employees) and *R.* v. *Trent Regional Health Authority, ex p. Jones, The Times* June 19, 1986 (where Macpherson J. held that judicial review was not available to challenge a decision to refuse employment to the applicant).

[49] *The Times*, March 8, 1986. See, similarly, *R.* v. *Independent Broadcasting Authority, ex p. Rank Organisation plc, The Times*, March 14, 1986 (Mann J.).

[50] Above note 7 at 418. See also *ex p. Molyneaux* [1986] 1 W.L.R. 331 (Taylor J.).

[51] *R.* v. *Monopolies and Mergers Commission, ex p. Argyll Group plc* [1986] 1 W.L.R. 763, at 774 (Sir John Donaldson M.R.).

[52] Based, of course, on the Court of Appeal judgment in *Associated Provincial Picture Houses Ltd.* v. *Wednesbury Corporation* [1948] 1 K.B. 223.

[53] See Lord Diplock in the G.C.H.Q. case on "the possible adoption in the future" of the European concept of proportionality: above note 7 at 410. See also *R.* v. *Brent L.B.C., ex p. Assegai The Times*, June 18, 1987 (Divisional Court).

[54] See the dissenting judgment of Lord Justice Browne-Wilkinson in the Court of Appeal in *Wheeler* v. *Leicester City Council* [1985] A.C. 1054 at 1061–1066.

Legitimate Expectation and Judicial Review

PATRICK ELIAS*

I. *The Concept of Legitimate Expectation*

One consequence of the development and increasing sophistication of public law concepts in the last twenty five years has been the expansion of judicial control over the administrative process. The courts have asserted the power to control not merely bodies exercising judicial or quasi-judicial functions affecting individual rights but also bodies exercising administrative functions affecting a wide variety of interests which do not constitute rights in the strict sense.[1] A central task of administrative law has been to define which interests should be afforded the protection of public law and which should not.

A concept which has been fashioned to help identify these interests deserving legal protection is the concept of legitimate expectation. This was first used by Lord Denning in the case of *Schmidt* v. *Secretary of State for Home Affairs*.[2] Schmidt was an alien who had been given leave to enter the United Kingdom and study scientology for a limited period. Once that period came to an end, Schmidt applied for an extension but this was refused by the Home Secretary without Schmidt being given the right to make representations. Schmidt sought a declaration that he ought to have been afforded a hearing. The Court of Appeal rejected this contention. Lord Denning M.R. enunciated the general principle as follows[3]:

> "The speeches in *Ridge* v. *Baldwin* [1964] A.C. 40 show that an administrative body may, in a proper case, be bound to give a person who is affected by their decision an opportunity of making representations. It all depends on whether he has some right

*The author would like to thank Simon Croall for his assistance in the preparation of this article.

or interest or, I would add, some legitimate expectation, of which it would not be fair to deprive him without hearing what he has to say." [Emphasis added]

Schmidt had no right or legitimate expectation because he had been allowed to remain for the period of time originally granted to him. But Lord Denning indicated that the position would have been otherwise had Schmidt's permit been revoked before the time had expired, for then he would have a legitimate expectation of being allowed to stay for the permitted time.

Since the *Schmidt* decision the concept has been employed in a wide variety of circumstances, not only by the English Courts but also in Commonwealth jurisdictions.[4] It was recognised by the House of Lords both in *O'Reilly* v. *Mackman*[5] and later in *In re Findlay*[6] that a legitimate expectation would found the basis of *locus standi* in judicial review proceedings. It was then adopted and applied by the House in *Council of Civil Service Unions* v. *Minister for the Civil Service*[7] (the *G.C.H.Q.* case). In that case the Minister issued instructions that the terms and conditions of service of staff at *G.C.H.Q.* should be varied so that they would no longer be permitted to belong to national trade unions. There was no consultation with the trade unions representing the staff notwithstanding a well established practice of consultation. The unions alleged that in failing to consult before such variations were effected the Minister had been in breach of her duty to act fairly. The House of Lords rejected this allegation on the grounds that on the facts interests of national security outweighed those of fairness. However, they unanimously agreed that, apart from considerations of national security, the invariable practice of consultation was such as to create a legitimate expectation that the unions would be consulted. In a very important judgment Lord Diplock took the opportunity to seek to define the concept of legitimate expectation in the context of analysing the proper ambit of judicial review. He did so as follows[8]:

"To qualify as a subject for judicial review the decision must have consequences which affect some person (or body of persons) other than the decision-maker, although it may affect him too. It must affect such other person either:

(a) by altering rights or obligations of that person which are enforceable by or against him in private law; or
(b) by depriving him of some benefit or advantage which either (i) he had in the past been permitted by the decision-maker to enjoy and which he can legitimately

expect to be permitted to continue to do until there has been communicated to him some rational grounds for withdrawing it on which he has been given an opportunity to comment; or (ii) he has received assurance from the decision-maker will not be withdrawn without giving him first an opportunity of advancing reasons for contending that they should not be withdrawn. (I prefer to continue to call the kind of expectation that qualifies a decision for inclusion in class (b) a 'legitimate expectation' rather than a 'reasonable expectation,' in order thereby to indicate that it has consequences to which effect will be given in public law, whereas an expectation or hope that some benefit or advantage would continue to be enjoyed, although it might be entertained by a 'reasonable' man, would not necessarily have such consequences.)"

The key feature of Lord Diplock's concept of legitimate expectation is that it focuses upon the conduct of the decision-maker. It is the expectation created by his conduct which creates the legitimate expectation which in turn provides the justification for judicial intervention.

This formulation helpfully distinguishes the two separate elements in the concept as developed by the courts. In some cases the legitimate expectation will be an expectation that a substantial benefit, privilege or other advantage will be conferred or continued. In other cases it will be the more limited expectation that no adverse decision affecting an individual will be taken without first affording that person the opportunity to make representations about it: the legitimate expectation is not that the benefit or advantage itself will ultimately be conferred. Furthermore, as Lord Fraser pointed out in the *G.C.H.Q.* case,[9] the expectation may be created by an express promise, or it may arise by implication from past practice. An example of an express promise creating the expectation is *Attorney General of Hong Kong* v. *Ng Yuen Shiu*[10] in which the Governor of Hong Kong had given certain assurances to illegal immigrants that they would only be deported after being interviewed, and that each case would be treated on its merits. The Privy Council granted prohibition against the execution of a removal order until a proper opportunity had been given to the applicant to enable him to make representations as to why he should not be deported. This was required in order for his case to be treated on its merits. The principle relied upon by the Privy Council was that it would be unfair and contrary to the interests of good administration for a public authority to act inconsistently with an undertaking or assurance it has given.[11]

The *G.C.H.Q.* case itself illustrates the situation where a legitimate expectation of consultation prior to a decision being reached arose by implication from past practice.[12] In contrast the case of *R.* v. *Board of Visitors of Hull Prison, ex p. St. Germain*,[13] a decision approved by the House of Lords in *O'Reilly* v. *Mackman*,[14] is an example of past practice creating an expectation of a substantive benefit or advantage. In that case the question was whether prisoners being subject to prison discipline could be found guilty of disciplinary offences without being given an opportunity to make representations. The effect of the disciplinary charge being sustained was that the prisoner might have to forfeit part of his remission. In normal circumstances a prisoner of good behaviour would have a remission of one third of his sentence. The Court of Appeal held that although the prisoner had no right to remission, nevertheless he had a privilege which ought to be protected in public law. In *O'Reilly* Lord Diplock referred to this as a legitimate expectation deriving from a well established practice. It would be unfair to frustrate that expectation without giving the prisoner an opportunity to make representations.

II. *Criticisms of Lord Diplock's Analysis*

This approval of the concept of legitimate expectation by the House of Lords is a significant development in administrative law. It ought to result in an extension of the boundaries of judicial review. It is submitted, however, that Lord Diplock's analysis, although in certain respects a valuable encapsulation of the principle, nevertheless distorts the true basis of judicial review. Moreover, if his analysis of the scope of judicial review is treated as exhaustive, it could even restrict the scope for such review.

The distortion arises from the fact that Lord Diplock uses the concept of legitimate expectation to embrace all those interests, other than rights strictly so called, which attract the protection of judicial review principles. This is not how Lord Denning originally formulated the concept. As we have seen, in *Schmidt*, he treated legitimate expectation cases as a species distinct both from rights and interests.[15] It is submitted that Lord Denning's analysis is preferable. Frequently the nature of the interest affected will of itself provide the justification for the application of judicial review principles, irrespective of the past conduct of the decision-maker. It is then misleading and unhelpful to focus upon the conduct of the decision-maker since, whilst this may well reinforce the justification for judicial review, it does not provide the principal foundation for it. It is the nature of the interest and not the fact that the person affected has been permitted to enjoy it by the decision-maker which justifies judicial protection. The notion that the nature of the interests at stake would justify the protection of judicial review principles was well established before the concept of legitimate expectation was developed. For example in *Durayappah* v. *Fernando*[16] the Privy Council held that in determining whether or not the principles of natural justice would apply to the protection of an individual's interests, factors to be taken into account should include the following: the nature of the complainant's interest; the circumstances in which it could be interfered with; and the sanction which might be imposed by the decision-maker. The expectation created by the conduct or behaviour of the decision-maker was not treated as a relevant factor. Moreover, by using the concept generically, Lord Diplock's analysis fails to bring out the special significance of the concept, namely the fact that in certain circumstances the interest adversely affected would not, absent the legitimate expectation, suffice to attract any protection from the principles of judicial review; it is then only the legitimate expectation arising out of the conduct of the decision-maker which provides the basis of protection. The *Hong Kong*[17] case provides a good illustration. There it was only the legitimate expectation arising from the assurance given by the Government that enabled the Court to intervene on behalf of the illegal immigrant: his status as an illegal immigrant would not of itself have created any entitlement to a hearing.

Furthermore, not all cases where judicial protection has in the past been afforded to the interests of individuals can satisfactorily be subsumed under Lord Diplock's concept of legitimate expectation. For example take the case of an adjoining landowner who is concerned about the effects of the granting of planning permission to a neighbour which might adversely affect his interests. It is widely accepted that fairness demands that he should be afforded an opportunity to make representations. But the requirements of fairness in this respect might conceivably be in direct conflict with the established practice of the planning authority.[18] In these circumstances it is not the conduct of the planning authority which has in any sense given rise to a legitimate expectation to make representations: fairness requires it irrespective of whether expectations have been created or not. Similarly an increase in taxi-cab licences may adversely affect the interests of existing cab drivers so as to justify their entitlement to make representations prior to the increase being made,[19] but it is artificial to say that the Licensing Authority has by its conduct in permitting them to have a licence thereby created an expectation that they will be consulted before new licences are granted. Moreover, the Court of Appeal has held that a refusal to grant a licence on an initial application may sometimes attract the safeguards of natural justice or fairness, yet there is no conceivable legitimate expectation in those circumstances.[20]

A recent example of the inappropriateness of seeking to subsume all non-rights cases under the umbrella of "legitimate expectation" is provided by *R.* v. *Secretary of State for Transport, ex p. Greater London Council*.[21] In that case the Secretary of State for Transport was empowered by the London Regional Transport Act 1984 *inter alia* to require the Greater London Council (G.L.C.) to make a payment by way of grant to London Regional Transport (L.R.T.). The relevant statute provided for a maximum amount that the G.L.C. could be required to pay. The G.L.C. successfully contended before McNeill J. that since the Secretary of State could direct that less than the maximum should be paid, it should be entitled to make representations to the Secretary of State as to how much should be paid. Accordingly the failure by the Secretary of State to permit such representations rendered his direction invalid. McNeill J. held that natural justice applied notwithstanding that, as he pointed out, it was not disputed that the G.L.C. had not previously enjoyed any benefit or privilege which it had been permitted by the Secretary of State to enjoy and could be expected to continue to enjoy. In short, no legitimate expectation was created in the sense discussed by Lord Diplock in the *G.C.H.Q.* case at all. Nevertheless the interests of the G.L.C. were sufficiently affected to warrant the protection of the principle of natural justice. On Lord Diplock's test, they should not have been entitled to make representations at all.

III. *Two Further Qualifications*

There are two other respects in which Lord Diplock's analysis needs qualification. First, Lord Diplock's formulation suggests that the legitimate expectation must arise from the way in which the individual affected by a decision has personally been dealt with in the past, or as a result of assurances given to him personally. This is not so. It is clear from the authorities that the expectation may arise from the way in which individuals in the same class or category as the individual affected have been treated in the past, or because of assurances given to that class as a whole, and not merely from treatment meted out to him personally. For example, a prisoner has a legitimate expectation that he will gain remission for good behaviour because that is the policy applied to prisoners: it may never in fact have been applied to him personally if, for example, he has never been in prison before.[22] Again, in the *Hong Kong* case the assurance was to illegal immigrants as a class, and not to any particular individual.

Secondly, Lord Diplock draws a sharp distinction between public and private law and suggests that the concept of legitimate expectation has no role in the latter sphere but is purely a public law concept. This is misleading since the concept has been applied to private bodies exercising public functions. For example in *Breen* v. *Amalgamated Union of Engineering Workers*[23] Lord Denning held that a person who was elected to the position of Shop Steward by his workmates but could not under the union's rules take up the position until the appointment had been ratified by the union's District Committee had a legitimate expectation that the appointment would be so ratified. Accordingly ratification could be refused only after he had been given the opportunity to make representations as to why his election should be confirmed. It was, said Lord Denning, an implied term in the contract of membership that the member would be treated fairly.[24] In this way the public law concept of legitimate expectation was given effect through the private law mechanism of contractual implied terms. Again in *McInnes* v. *Onslow Fane*[25] Megarry J. held that the British Boxing Board of Control, a private association that effectively controlled the training and managing of boxers by issuing licences, was under a duty to act fairly and that this would embrace an obligation to give a hearing to a person whose licence was for some reason not being renewed. He would have a legitimate expectation of renewal, and such an expectation should not be frustrated without proper cause and after a hearing. Since the British Boxing Board of Control is a private association it is questionable whether it could be the subject of proceedings brought under Order 53,[26] but in a suitable case Megarry J. clearly envisaged that at least a declaration could be sought. Accordingly it seems that the Courts will fashion techniques to ensure that private law bodies exercising public functions will in some circumstances be subject to public law principles, including the doctrine of legitimate expectation. To that extent the doctrine is not purely a creature of public law.

IV. *A Theoretical Problem*

Brennan J. in the Australian High Court has adopted an interesting position as to the significance of the doctrine of legitimate expectation. He has argued that whilst it may influence the content of natural justice in particular circumstances, it cannot have any relevance to the prior question of whether natural justice is in principle applicable. In *Kioa* v. *West* he expressed his reasons for adopting this view as follows[27]:

> "But the expectation of an individual whose interests may be affected by an exercise of a power is not relevant to the construction of the statute which creates the power. The construction to be placed on the statute cannot depend on whether an individual has an expectation that the power will be exercised in his favour or that he will be consulted and given an opportunity to put a case before the power will be exercised against him. It is not the state of mind of an individual but the interest which an exercise of power is apt to affect that is relevant to the construction of the statute. A 'legitimate expectation' cannot arise unless an exercise of the power is capable of affecting, for good or ill, the interests of the person who holds that expectation. Lord Fraser of Tullybelton in C.C.S.U. (at 401) identified the circumstances which give rise to a legitimate or reasonable expectation as either 'an express promise given on behalf of a public authority or . . . . . . the existence of a regular practice which the claimant can reasonably expect to continue.' When either of those circumstances occur it may be unfair not to give a hearing to the person to whom the promise was made or who has relied on the practice, but neither the promise nor the practice is relevant to the legislature's intention to condition the exercise of power by the public authority on its observance of the principles of natural justice. Those circumstances may be relevant to what is required to satisfy the principles of natural justice in particular circumstances."

It is submitted that His Honour was correct to emphasise that it is generally the nature of the interest affected rather than any expectation which might have been engendered which will determine whether or not the principles of natural justice are applicable. However, he was wrong to assert that the concept of legitimate expectation cannot in any circumstances provide the basis for incorporating the principles of natural justice. The theoretical difficulty he raises is essentially this: that the right to be afforded natural justice must arise from the proper construction of the relevant statute, and that the construction cannot vary depending upon the expectation of individuals. Both limbs in the argument are, with respect, fallacious. As to the first, the theory that all principles of judicial review have their basis in the presumed intentions of Parliament—the fiction that the courts are merely acting as the handmaidens of Parliament in imposing principles or standards of judicial review—has been exploded by the *G.C.H.Q.* case itself. For there the House of Lords held that prerogative powers are in principle reviewable. Since these powers are not derived from Parliament, the justification for reviewing them cannot be based upon the presumed intentions of Parliament. It can only be that it is the common law itself which is providing the principles of review, subject always of course to their not conflicting with any contrary intentions expressed by Parliament. On this analysis it is the common law which imposes the obligation to permit representations to be made before expectations are frustrated.[28] Parliament's intentions are relevant only insofar as they may in particular circumstances restrict the operation of common law principles.

As to the second limb, even if the application of natural justice does depend upon the presumed intentions of Parliament, there is no reason why the presumption should not be that Parliament intends the decision-maker to act fairly in exercising the powers conferred upon him,[29] and that fairness may in some, but not all, circumstances require that a hearing should be given. There is no reason to suppose that Parliament would either have intended that natural justice should always be applicable, when a particular power is being exercised, or that it should never be. Yet this appears to be the logic of Brennan J.'s position.

V. *A purely procedural concept?*

In most cases where the concept of legitimate expectation has been employed it has been used for the purpose of invoking the

principles of natural justice. But does it merely attract procedural safeguards or can it go further and be relied upon to
attract substantive principles of review? The answer will
depend upon how the concept of legitimate expectation is
being defined. If it embraces all interests which may be protected by judicial review other than rights strictly so called,
then obviously bodies which make decisions affecting those
interests will often be bound to respect the substantive principles of review (which include, but are not limited to, the *Wednesbury* grounds). This was recognised by Lord Diplock in the
case of *O'Reilly* v. *Mackman* when he said; in relation to the
expectation of prisoners to a remission of their sentence[30]:

> "In public law, as distinguished from private law ... such
> legitimate expectation gave to each appellant a sufficient
> interest to challenge the adverse disciplinary award made
> against him ... on the ground that in one way or another
> the board in reaching its decision had acted out with the
> powers conferred on it by the legislation under which it
> was acting; and such grounds would include the board's
> failure ... to act fairly towards him in carrying out the
> decision making process."

However, where the concept of legitimate expectation is
used merely to denote an expectation flowing from an assurance or representation by the decision-maker, the position
appears to be more complex. Where the assurance is merely
that a hearing will be granted, then logically that justifies a
complaint only on the ground that such a hearing is denied
without good cause. But suppose an assurance or undertaking
is given about the way in which the decision-maker will exercise power or discretion, such as commonly occurs in government circulars or statements of policy. Can a person require
the decision-maker to act only in accordance with that assurance or undertaking?

In general the answer must be that he cannot. It is a well
established principle of administrative law that a public body
cannot fetter its future executive action by contract or estoppel.[31]
Moreover, it is clear that no person can make a claim arising out of
the frustration of his expectations which results from a change of
policy adopted by a public body.[32] Such expectations, although
they may have been reasonably held, do not constitute "legitimate
expectations" so as to attract the safeguards of judicial review
principles. This point is well illustrated by the decision of the

House of Lords in *In re Findlay*.[33] In that case the Home Office altered the policy relating to the remission of sentences for certain categories of prisoner. An affected prisoner alleged that he should have been consulted prior to the change on the grounds that he had a legitimate expectation that he would receive the benefits conferred by the policy. Lord Scarman giving judgment for the House of Lords, rejected this contention in the following terms[34]:

> "But what was their legitimate expectation? Given the substance and purpose of the legislative provisions governing parole, the most that a convicted prisoner can legitimately expect is that his case will be examined individually in the light of whatever policy the Secretary of State sees fit to adopt provided always that the adopted policy is a lawful exercise of the discretion conferred upon him by the statute. Any other view would entail the conclusion that the unfettered discretion conferred by the statute upon the minister can in some cases be restricted so as to hamper, or even to prevent changes of policy."

Nevertheless in certain limited circumstances the courts have shown that they are willing to hold public bodies to undertakings or assurances given. In *R*. v. *Inland Revenue Commissioners, ex p. Preston*[35] the Revenue agreed with a taxpayer that they would make no further demands for tax if the taxpayer relinquished claims to various tax reliefs. Subsequently the Revenue made a demand of the taxpayer when it was too late for the taxpayer to claim the reliefs. The taxpayer sought judicial review of this on the grounds, *inter alia*, that the Revenue had acted unfairly in the circumstances in resiling from its undertaking. On the facts the House of Lords held that there was no unfairness: the taxpayer had not disclosed all relevant facts to the Revenue when the original agreement was reached, and in the circumstances the Revenue was not acting unfairly in making the demand afresh. However their Lordships accepted that in principle it would in certain situations be an improper exercise of power for a public body to refuse to honour undertakings or assurances it has given. Lord Templeman, with whose judgment the other Lords concurred, held that resiling from an undertaking would normally constitute an abuse of power if the conduct would, if committed by a private body, have given rise to a claim for breach of contract or estoppel by representation.[36] His Lordship accepted, however, that there may be circumstances in which such conduct did not constitute unfairness meriting review, although he did not indicate precisely what those circumstances would be.

Preston was a case involving an assurance to an individual taxpayer where reliance upon the assurance resulted in prejudice to the applicant. In contrast in *R.* v. *Secretary of State for the Home Office, ex p. Kahn*[37] the Court of Appeal held that the Home Office was bound by a circular directed to the public at large and not any specific individuals, even though there was no prejudicial reliance on it. In that case a Pakistani couple settled in England wished to adopt a child living in Pakistan. A Home Office circular specified the circumstances in which the Home Secretary would exceptionally exercise his discretion to allow a child to be brought into the United Kingdom for such adoption. The circular indicated that the discretion would be exercised if four conditions were satisfied. An application for entry clearance for the child was turned down for a reason not specified in the circular. The Court of Appeal held by a majority that this refusal by the Secretary of State was ultra vires: the Home Secretary had acted unfairly and in breach of the applicant's legitimate expectations. Parker L.J. held that "the Secretary of State, if he undertakes to allow in persons if certain conditions are satisfied, should not in my view be entitled to resile from that undertaking without affording interested persons a hearing and then only if the overriding public interest demands it,"[38] echoing similar sentiments expressed by Lord Denning in the *Liverpool Taxis* case.[39] Even in the absence of detrimental reliance, the public interest requires the undertaking to be honoured unless there are strong countervailing public policy considerations. Parker L.J. even went so far as to say that a new policy could only be adopted vis-a-vis a recipient of the letter after considering whether an overriding public interest required it. It is difficult, however, to reconcile this with the observations of Lord Scarman made in the *Findlay* case, which are reproduced above. Dunn L.J. agreed with Parker L.J. that the Home Secretary had acted unfairly, but he adopted a different analysis, namely that the circular effectively defined the ambit of relevant considerations which the Home Secretary could consider, so that by taking into account any additional factors he was taking into account irrelevant factors. This differs from Parker L.J.'s analysis in one crucial respect: it means that in effect the Home Secretary is estopped from departing from the circular, notwithstanding Dunn L.J.'s protestations to the contrary. It is virtually impossible to reconcile this approach with the principle that a public body cannot fetter its powers either by policy or by estoppel. In contrast, Parker L.J.'s analysis would not ultimately mean that a public authority was bound by its representations, since it can always depart from them where there is a strong counter-vailing public interest. If this were not so, a public authority might be reluctant to adopt and publish general policies at all.[40]

These developments are to be welcomed. They do, however, mean that public bodies have to tread a fine line. On the one hand they must not treat themselves as bound by policy guidelines[41], on the other they must not readily depart from such guidelines. They still have an overriding obligation to exercise their powers in the public interest, but an important element in determining where the public interest lies is the fact that undertakings or assurances should in general be honoured. In this way the courts have adopted principles which enable them to balance considerations of fairness with wider aspects of the public interest.

Notes

[1] These cases have been fully documented elsewhere; see Wade, *Administrative Law* (1982), pp. 464–465; Craig, *Administrative Law* (1983), pp. 260–261 and J.M. Evans, *de Smith's Judicial Review of Adminstrative Action* (1980), p. 177.

[2] [1969] 2 Ch. 149.

[3] *ibid.* note 2 at 170.

[4] See in particular: *Heatley* v. *Tasmanian Racing and Gaming Commission* (1977) 137 C.L.R. 487; *F.A.I. Insurances Ltd.* v. *Winneke* (1982) 56 A.L.J.R. 388; *Salemi* v. *Minister for Immigration and Ethnic Affairs* (No.2) (1977) 137 C.L.R. 396; *R.* v. *MacKellar, ex p. Ratu* (1977) 137 C.L.R. 461; *Smitty's Industries* v. *Attorney General* [1980] 1 N.Z.L.R. 355. For a general discussion see D.C. Hodgson, 14 Melbourne Univ. L.R. 686 and also Graeme Johnson, (1985) 15 *Federal Law Review* 39.

[5] [1983] 2 A.C. 237.

[6] [1985] A.C. 318.

[7] [1985] A.C. 374.

[8] *ibid.* note 7 at 408–409. In *R.* v. *Secretary of State for the Environment, ex p. Nottinghamshire C.C.* (1986) 2 W.L.R. 1 at 6 Lord Scarman referred to this analysis as a classical "but certainly not exhaustive analysis."

[9] *ibid.* note 7 at 401.

[10] [1983] 2 A.C. 629

[11] See the language of Lord Denning M.R. in *R.* v. *Liverpool Corporation ex p. Liverpool Taxi Fleet Operators' Association* [1972] 2 Q.B. 299 and of Scarman L.J. in *H.T.V. Ltd.* v. *Price Commission* [1976] I.C.R. 170, C.A.

[12] See also the decision of Hodgson J. in *R.* v. *Brent London Borough Council, ex p. Gunning* (1985) 84 L.G.R. 168.

[13] [1979] Q.B. 425.

[14] *ibid.* note 5 at 274.

¹⁵ It is arguably more accurate to say that legitimate expectations are simply one category of interest rather than a category distinct from rights or interests.

¹⁶ [1967] 2 A.C. 337.

¹⁷ *ibid.* note 10.

¹⁸ See *Buxton* v. *Minister of Housing and Local Government* [1961] 1 Q.B. 278.

¹⁹ See *R.* v. *Liverpool Corporation, ex parte Liverpool Taxi Fleet Operators' Association* [1972] 2 Q.B. 299 at 308: There was in fact an express undertaking to consult in that case, but Lord Denning's judgment indicates that he considered that fairness would have required consultation in any event: the undertaking merely confirmed the common law position.

²⁰ *R.* v. *Gaming Board for Great Britain, ex p. Benaim and Khaida* [1970] 2 Q.B. 417 (but contrast the decision of Megarry V.C. in *McInnes* v. *Onslow Fane* [1978] 1 W.L.R. 1520).

²¹ [1986] Q.B. 556

²² See in particular *O'Reilly* v. *Mackman* [1983] 2 A.C. 217 at 275.

²³ [1971] 2 Q.B. 175.

²⁴ *ibid.* at 190.

²⁵ *ibid.* note 20.

²⁶ However the decision of the Court of Appeal in *R.* v. *Panel on Takeovers and Mergers, ex p. Datafin* [1987] Q.B. 815 indicates that a private body exercising a public function may be susceptible to judicial review.

²⁷ [1986] 60 A.L.J.R. 113 at 142.

²⁸ There is respected old authority that the right to natural justice arises from the common law: See *Cooper* v. *Wandsworth Board of Works* (1863) 14 C.B.(N.S.) 180.

²⁹ This presumption has been relied on by the House of Lords on several occasions; see *Pearlberg* v. *Varty* [1972] 1 W.L.R. 534; *Wiseman* v. *Borneman* [1971] A.C. 297.

³⁰ ibid note at page 275.

³¹ See in particular on fettering by estoppel *Western Fish Products Ltd.* v. *Penwith D.C.* [1981] 2 All E.R. 204, and in general Wade, *Administrative Law* (1982) pp. 141–146.

³² See e.g. *Laker Airways Ltd.* v. *Department of Trade* [1977] Q.B. 643 and *In re Findlay ibid.* note 6.

³³ *ibid.* note 6.

³⁴ *ibid.* note 6 at 388.

³⁵ [1985] A.C. 835. For a valuable note on this case and the wider issues discussed in the text, see Clive Lewis (1986) 49 M.L.R. 251.

³⁶ *ibid.* note 35 at 866; See too, the Court of Appeal decision in *Gowa and Others* v. *A.G., The Times,* December 27, 1984, where the citizenship was granted by estoppel. The House of Lords resolved the issue on other grounds: [1985] 1 W.L.R. 1003. But see also *H.T.V.* v. *Price Commission* [1976] I.C.R. 170, a case relied upon in *Preston,* where the Court of Appeal stated that the reliance need have no detrimental effect to the complainant.

³⁷ [1984] 1 W.L.R. 1337. See note by Alistair R. Mowbray, [1985] P.L. 558; See *R.* v. *Secretary of State for the Home Department, ex p. Ruddock* [1987] 2 All E.R. 518.

³⁸ *ibid.* note 37 at 1344.

³⁹ See *R.* v. *Liverpool Corporation, ex p. Liverpool Taxi Fleet Operators Association* [1972] 2 Q.B. 299 at 308.

⁴⁰ Though see the observations of Lord Scarman in the *Findlay* case to the effect that it would sometimes be impossible for a body to exercise its duties without adopting a policy, [1985] 1 A.C. 318 at 335.

⁴¹ See e.g. *British Oxygen Co. Ltd.* v. *Board of Trade* [1971] A.C. 610 and *R.* v. *Port of London Authority, ex p. Kynoch* [1919] 1 K.B. 176.

Proportionality: Neither Novel Nor Dangerous

JEFFREY JOWELL AND ANTHONY LESTER Q.C.*

I. *Introduction*

Lord Diplock, in the *G.C.H.Q.* case[1] usefully classified three grounds of judicial review of administrative action[2] and tantalisingly alluded to a possible fourth ground, that of "proportionality." In an earlier case Lord Diplock, though not referring directly to proportionality, counselled against the use of a "steamhammer to crack a nut."[3] More recently however Mr. Justice Millett called the "now fashionable" concept of proportionality "a novel and dangerous doctrine" and declined to apply it as a test of the validity of a covenant in restraint of trade.[4]

In this essay we argue that proportionality is by no means novel. It has been employed, often under other names, in a number of areas of English law. Far from being dangerous, it embodies a basic principle of fairness, the explicit recognition of which would, we believe, greatly strengthen the coherence of our developing system of administrative law.

Proportionality, as a recognised general principle of law originated in Germany and has more recently been adopted in France and other member states of the European Economic Community. We begin this essay by briefly sketching the use of proportionality in Germany and France. We then give examples of its application by the Court of Justice of the European Communities and as a general principle in the interpretation of the European Convention of Human Rights. A resolution of the Committee of Ministers of the Council of Europe, adopted on March 11, 1980, recommended governments of member states to be guided in their law and

* The authors are grateful for the assistance in the preparation of this essay from Professor Albert Kiralfy, Roger Errera, Francis Snyder, Carol Harlow and Ross Denton, none of whom is responsible for its deficiencies.

administrative practice by various principles annexed to the resolution. One of those principles contains the notion of proportionality requiring an administrative authority when exercising a discretionary power to

> "maintain a proper balance between any adverse effects which its decision may have on the rights, liberties or interests of persons and the purpose which it pursues."

In a recent case[5] Mr. Justice Schiemann referred to that resolution because of its acceptance by the United Kingdom and used the principle of proportionality to test the reasonableness of the government's suspension of the permits of Romanian pilots. In the last part of this essay we consider the extent to which this principle of proportionality has already been applied in English public law. We argue that it is not alien to common law concepts, and suggest that the time is ripe explicitly to recognise it as a general principle of judicial review.

II. *Proportionality in German Law*

German administrative law requires administrative acts to be exercised in accordance with the principle of *Verhältnismässigkeit*.[6] The principle originated in the late nineteenth century when it was invoked by the Prussian Supreme Administrative Court to check the discretionary powers of police authorities.[7] Since then the principle has acquired a constitutional status and applies to legislative as well as judicial acts. It is regarded as a consequence of the *Rechtsstaat* or Constitutional State, under which state power may only encroach upon individual freedom to the extent that it is indispensable for the protection of the public interest.[8]

The principle of *Verhältnismässigkeit* contains three interconnected and overlapping conditions, each of which must be satisfied for the validity of an administrative action. These conditions are suitability, necessity and proportionality (narrowly defined).

(i) The principle of suitability

This principle requires authorities to employ means which are appropriate to the accomplishment of a given law, and which are not in themselves incapable of implementation or unlawful. For example, an administrative direction requiring the installation of a plant on a site where the qualities of the land make its construction impossible has been held unlawful.[9] A tenant cannot be required to make alterations in a building under his tenancy;[10] and the police may not require the owner of kennels to reduce noise by keeping the dogs in closed rooms, in a manner inconsistent with the law relating to the protection of animals.[11]

(ii) The principle of necessity

This principle requires that the least harmful of more than one available means be adopted to achieve a particular objective. Like the United States principle of the "less restrictive alternative,"[12] German law requires public bodies to pursue those regulatory measures which cause the minimum injury to an individual or community. An innkeeper should not be fined if the regulation of the noise from his premises could be effectively controlled by advancing his closing hours.[13] The principle of necessity only applies however where more than one means is available to implement the law's objective.

(iii) The principle of proportionality (in the narrow sense)

Here the courts engage in a balancing exercise between the injury to individual rights caused by an administrative measure and the corresponding gain to the community. The German courts require proof of manifest or clear disproportionality before they will substitute their own opinion for the opinion of the legislator or administrator on the merits of the weight to be accorded to either side of the equation. For example, the German courts have not been willing to prevent the demolition of an unlawful construction as violating the principle of proportionality.[14] However, when authorities refused to issue a character reference to a person against whom criminal proceedings were pending, the court held that the refusal violated the principle of proportionality, since the failure to provide the reference contravened the plaintiff's right to pursue a vocation of his choice. In the circumstances of that case the violation was held disproportionately to outweigh any consequential benefits to society.[15]

The principle of proportionality has been applied in cases involving the expulsion of foreigners following their criminal conviction. In one case the court considered that the expulsion of a foreigner, following a particularly violent crime, was justified[16]; in other cases the expulsions following convictions for minor traffic violations were held to be unlawful.[17] The Federal Administrative Court has laid down relevant criteria governing the decision to expel, including the nature of the offence, the foreigner's length of stay, extent of his integration, contacts in his native land, overall behaviour, etc.[18] The courts have also required that, in considering the losses to the individual against the gain to the community, public authorities must also take into account the incidental effects of their expulsion on third parties.[19]

III. *Proportionality in French Law*

Writing in 1974, Guy Braibant, the distinguished member of the Conseil d'Etat,[20] welcomed the recent application of the concept of proportionality in international administrative law through a case of the International Labour Tribunal, striking down a decision of the International Labour Bureau to dismiss one of their sleeping nightwatchmen. Braibant noted the acceptance of proportionality as a general principle of law in German and Swiss law, and urged its overt recognition in French law.

Braibant considered the principle to endorse a "rule of common sense," that one ought not to "shoot a swallow with a cannon" or, to use a more common French expression, "to crush a fly with a sledgehammer." He pointed out that the principle was more complex than a simple requirement that means justify the ends, but required a reasonable relation between a decision, its objective, and the circumstances in which the decision was taken. Thus understood, proportionality was not confined to cases involving a decision to penalise an individual, but also applied to decisions about economic and social ends.

Braibant went on to examine situations in which the concept of proportionality, although not often expressed as such, was nevertheless applied:

> "Even where the concept is not expressly stated, it is beneath the surface. The French administrative judge, in short, applies the principle of proportionality without knowing or, more accurately, without saying so."[21]

The time had come, said Braibant, to be explicit about the principle, and to classify the situations in which it would apply.

The examples of the application of the principle of proportionality given by Braibant included the exercise of police powers, where the courts had annulled the prohibition of public meetings on the ground that the threat of a breach of peace was not sufficiently serious to justify interference with freedom of expression.[22] In the area of pollution control, French courts have required the relevant authority to ensure that the benefit to the public interest by ordering the closure of a polluting plant was balanced by the damage to the 'economic and social order' that would follow from the closure.[23] In the setting of fees or tolls by public authorities Braibant cited cases of the courts requiring a reasonable relationship between the amount charged and the service provided.[24] Public expenditure by local authorities (or communes)—for example for the construction of an airport—had been held unlawful where it was out of proportion to the authority's financial resources.[25]

The principle of proportionality is firmly established in the area of disciplinary sanctions imposed upon civil servants[26] where penalties that are so disproportionate to the offence have been held unlawful on the ground of *"erreur manifeste d'appréciation des faits"* (manifest error in the assessment of facts—referred to simply as *erreur manifeste*—and the rough equivalent to our *"Wednesbury* unreasonableness" or "irrationality").[27]

An important development of the proportionality doctrine in France arose out of a decision of the Conseil d'Etat of which M. Braibant himself was a member in the case of *Ville Nouvelle Est*.[28] In that case compulsory purchase procedures were set in motion to acquire a huge site for a single residential and academic complex for the University of Lille. The scheme was approved by the minister as being in the public interest, but it was challenged by local associations. The Conseil d'Etat upheld the minister's decision on the ground that his decision was warranted by sufficient evidence. The decision, however, was notable for M. Braibant's statement requiring the carrying out of a balance of costs and benefits (*le bilan coût-avantages*).[29] Without interfering in the merits (opportunité) of the decision, he stated that the minister could not declare an operation to be in the public interest unless

> "the interference with private property, the financial cost, and, where they arise, the attendant social inconveniences are not excessive having regard to the needs of the operation."[30]

Following the *Ville Nouvelle Est* case the doctrine of *le bilan* has become established, at least in the area of planning and compensation law. For example, variation from a zoning regulation was struck down because of absence of proper proportion between regard to the public interest in maintaining the zoning and allowing it to be varied.[31] The construction of a slip-road off an autoroute was held unlawful because regard had not been had to the interests of the inmates of a psychiatric hospital who would be disturbed by the use of the road on that site.[32]

IV. *Proportionality in European Community Law*

The European Court of Justice has developed what Wyatt & Dashwood[33] refer to as "common law" principles, based upon the laws of Member States, by which the Court evaluates the legality of acts of the Community institutions. A distinction is drawn between "general principles of law" and "fundamental rights," although there is overlap between the two. Proportionality is now clearly established as a general principle of law.[34] In *Internationale Handelsgesellschaft*[35] the principle was defined as requiring that "the individual should not have his freedom of action limited beyond the degree necessary for the public interest."

Article 78(3) of the EEC Treaty subjects the requirements of free movement of workers to exceptions justified on grounds of public policy, public security or public health. In *Rutili* v. *French Minister of the Interior*[36] an Italian resident in France who had allegedly indulged in subversive activities was issued with a residence permit subject to a prohibition on residence in certain departments. The Court held that the exceptions in Article 78(3) to the right to the free movement of workers must be interpreted strictly, and that interference with this right could be justified only by a "genuine and sufficiently serious threat to public policy necessary for the protection of those interests in a democratic society." The terms of the permit could not be so justified and thus violated the test of proportionality.

Article 43(2) of the EEC Treaty provides that the Council of Ministers shall take steps to implement the common agricultural policy (set out in Article 39). The principle of proportionality is one ground of review of the Council's action (the other main one is the principle of non-discrimination) and is also mentioned explicitly in the context of Article 40(3) which provides that common organisations "may include all measures required to obtain the objectives set out in Article 39."

In *Bela-Muhle Josef Bergmann* v. *Grows-Farm*[37] an attack was made on the Council's Regulation 563/76[38] which made compulsory the use of skimmed milk power in the feeding of livestock. The purpose of the regulation was to reduce surpluses of skimmed milk powder but its effect was to make the cost to users three times that of the equivalent amount of vegetable feeding stuffs. On references from German and Dutch courts, the Court held that the measures went above and beyond what was necessary to attain the objective of diminishing the surpluses of skimmed milk powder.

Another area where proportionality is applied in Community Law is under Articles 30 and 34 of the Treaty, relating to the prohibition against quantitative restrictions and measures having equivalent effect on imports and exports. Article 36 of the Treaty allows certain restrictions if justified on various grounds, including "public morality, public policy or public security (and) the protection of health and life of humans," provided that such measures do not constitute "means of arbitrary discrimination or a disguised restriction on trade between Member States."

In *de Peijper*[39] the Court invoked the principle of proportionality to hold that restrictive provisions of imports in the Dutch legislation for the protection of health and life of humans would not fall within the exceptions under Article 36 if the same objective could be achieved by means less restrictive of intra-Community trade.

The principle of proportionality has also been invoked by the Court, for example, in interpreting the Community principles of equal treatment and of equal pay without sex discrimination. In *Johnston* v. *Chief Constable*[40] the Court stated[41] that

> "in determining the scope of any derogation from an individual right such as the equal treatment of men and women . . . the principle of proportionality, one of the general principles underlying the Community legal order, must be observed. That principle requires that derogations remain within the limits of what is appropriate and necessary for achieving the aim in view."

In *Bilka-Kaufhaus GmbH.* v. *Weber von Hartz*[42] the Court stated[43] that, under Article 119 of the EEC Treaty, an employer may justify the adoption of a pay policy excluding part-time workers, irrespective of their sex, from its occupational pension scheme on the ground that it seeks to employ as few part-time workers as possible,

> "where it is found that the means chosen for achieving that objective correspond to a real need on the part of the undertaking, are appropriate with a view to achieving the objective in question and are necessary to that end."

In both cases, the rights in question are directly effective in domestic law. Accordingly, United Kingdom courts and tribunals are under a duty to apply the principle of proportionality. Indeed, so much was recognised by the House of Lords, when approving the *Bilka-Kaufhaus* test in *Rainey* v. *Greater Glasgow Health Board*.[44] To the extent that Community law is directly effective, the principle of proportionality has been directly incorporated into the laws of the United Kingdom.[45]

V. *Proportionality under the European Convention*

Proportionality has also frequently been used as a general principle of law to interpret the provisions of the European Convention on Human Rights.[46] Even where an interference with a fundamental right pursues a legitimate aim, the means employed must be reasonably related to the pursuit of that aim. For example, Article 10(1) of the Convention guarantees the right to freedom of expression and the right to receive and impart information and ideas "without interference by public authority." These rights may be limited under Article 10(2) by,

> "such formalities, conditions, restrictions or penalties as are prescribed by law and are necessary in a democratic society, in the interests of national security, territorial integrity or public safety, for the prevention of disorder or crime, for the protection of health or morals, for the protection of the reputation of rights of others, for preventing the disclosure of information received in confidence, or for maintaining the authority and impartiality of the judiciary."

In the *Sunday Times* (Thalidomide) case,[47] the "necessity" of the House of Lords' injunction preventing the publication and dissemination of an article and information about pending Thalidomide litigation was examined using the test of proportionality. The Strasbourg Court had to decide whether the "interference" complained of corresponded to a "pressing social need" and was "proportionate to the legitimate aim pursued" and in particular "necessary" in a democratic society to protect the authority of the judiciary. The Court held that the restraint imposed upon the applicants' freedom of expression "proves not to be proportionate to the legitimate aim pursued; it was not necessary in a democratic society for maintaining the authority of the judiciary."[48]

In *Lithgow & Others*,[49] the Court considered the adequacy of compensation paid to shipbuilding companies for the taking of their property under United Kingdom nationalisation legislation, in the light of Article 1 of the First Protocol to the European Convention. The Court stated that a measure depriving a person of his property must pursue a legitimate aim in the public interest and that "there must also be a reasonable relationship of proportionality between the means employed and the aim sought to be realised."[50] The principle of proportionality had been expressed in an earlier case, *Sporrong & Lonroth*[51] in terms of the concept of "fair balance" required to be struck between the demands of the general interest of the community and the protection of the individual's fundamental rights. It was held in that case that such a balance would not be found if the person concerned had to bear "an individual and excessive burden."[52] In *Lithgow*, the Court observed that

> "Clearly, compensation terms are material to the assessment whether a fair balance has been struck between various interests at stake and, notably, whether or not a disproportionate burden has been imposed on the person who has been deprived of his possessions."[53]

In evaluating the adequacy of compensation the Court stated that the taking of property without payment of an amount "reasonably related" to its value would normally constitute a "disproportionate interference" with property rights.[54]

VI. *Proportionality in English Law*

In the absence of explicit guarantees of positive rights or a codified set of administrative law principles, English law has traditionally preferred to deal in remedies rather than principles.[55] Our judges have been reluctant to express basic notions of fairness as fundamental principles of law. The now hallowed concept of "natural justice" was narrowly applied for a long period, and even now is frequently disowned as excessively vague, and even "romantic."[56] The notion that public officials should exercise a sense of proportion fits clearly with traditional English concepts of justice, yet, true to another tradition, judges have gone to lengths to disguise the principle in the language of pragmatism.[57] All the same, the principle has been applied, and has recently been openly acknowledged.

Proportionality is most obviously applied where a punishment bears a disproportionate relationship to an offence. The Bill of Rights of 1689 forbids "excessive baile . . . excessive fines" and "cruell and unusuall punishments."[58] Reference was made to those prohibitions recently by Lord Justice Purchas in relation to the conduct of a prison governor.[59] It is well established in the criminal law that the punishment must fit the crime in the sense of being proportionate to the gravity of the offence.[60] The notion of an excessive condition of bail, or an excessive fine, or of a punishment which is cruel or unusual are deeply rooted in English attitudes towards impermissible state action: that the means employed should be reasonably related or proportionate to the actions of the state or public authorities. In relation to violent offences against the person, it is trite law that force used in self defence must bear a proportionate relation to the danger posed by the attack.

In *R. v. Barnsley M.B.C., ex p. Hook*[61] the Barnsley Corporation suspended a stallholder's licence because he had been guilty of misconduct when he urinated in the street and used offensive language. The Court of Appeal struck down the suspension on the ground of the lack of a fair hearing. Lord Denning MR however would also have intervened on the ground that "the punishment is altogether excessive and out of proportion to the occasion."[62] In *R. v. Secretary of State for the Home Department, ex p. Benwell,*[63] Hodgson J. accepted that "in an extreme case an administrative or quasi-judicial penalty can be successfully attacked on the ground that it was so disproportionate to the offence as to be perverse."[64]

Local authorities have recently imposed severe penalties of a variety of kinds upon individuals for a variety of reasons. In *Wheeler v. Leicester City Council,*[65] the Council withdrew the licence of a local rugby club to use a Council-owned practice groundbecause the club had refused to press four members who had agreed to take part in the English rugby footballers' tour of South Africa to withdraw from that tour. The Council was acting in pursuance of their statutory power (to grant licences on their own land) and claimed that they were acting also under their general statutory duty (under Section 71 of the Race Relations Act 1976) to promote good race relations. The House of Lords held the action to be unlawful, Lord Templeman considering it to be a misuse of power, "punishing the Club where it had done no wrong." Lord Roskill considered the withdrawal of a licence to be an unfair means of pursuing the council's ends. Both speeches, without specifically using the term, reflect the notion of disproportionality, Lord Templeman concentrating on the lack of relation between the penalty and any wrong, Lord Roskill concentrating on the lack of relation between the penalty and the council's legitimate objectives.

Lord Templeman supported his reasoning by reference to *Congreve* v. *Home Office*,[66] where the Home Secretary's actions in withdrawing television licences from those who had failed to pay a higher fee but were nevertheless within their rights so to do was considered by the Court of Appeal to be an unlawful punishment because it related to no wrong.

At the heart of both *Congreve* and *Wheeler* was the refusal of the court to countenance the achievement of a legitimate end (the raising of revenue in *Congreve* and the promotion of good race relations in *Wheeler*) by disproportionate means (punishing, in each case, where the individual had done no legal wrong).

More recently, Brent London Borough Council excluded a member of the public from local authority property on the ground of his unacceptable behaviour at various private meetings. The Divisional Court held the council's actions to be unlawful not only because of the absence of a fair hearing but also, in the words of Lord Justice Woolf, because

> "The banning resolution was in very wide terms and constituted a reaction wholly out of proportion to what the applicant had done."[67]

English courts are naturally reluctant to interfere with the Home Secretary's wide discretion to deport an alien.[68] Nevertheless the courts have made some attempt to require the exercise of a sense of proportion in cases where an alien has committed a criminal offence. Matters which the courts themselves take into account in recommending deportation include the seriousness of the offence in the light of other considerations such as the effect the deportation would have on innocent persons such as the offender's family.[69] In other words, the mere fact that a criminal offence has been committed should not of itself be a ground for deportation, and the courts attempt to ensure that the deportation bears a proportionate relationship to the offence in the light of other relevant considerations.

The principle of proportionality applies not only in cases where a penalty or punishment is in issue. It also arises in cases where a benefit is awarded but is not considered sufficient compensation for the related task. Thus where a retiring civil servant was awarded a derisory penny-a-year gratuity, the Privy Council held that the award was a mere pretence and amounted to a refusal to exercise the Board's discretion "reasonably, fairly and justly."[70] Further elucidation could have made clear that the award was in no way proportionate to the civil servant's past service and was for that reason unreasonable, unfair and unjust.

Similar artificial devices aimed at avoiding a statute's purposes have been struck down. For example, in *Backhouse* v. *Lambeth L.B.C.*[71] a housing authority, in order to avoid raising rents generally, charged the whole of the required increase in rents upon a single property. The court held this increase to be unlawful, focusing on the (disproportionate) increase in rent (from £7 to £18,000 per week) on the one property, despite the literal fulfillment of the statute's purpose.

In cases involving local authority expenditure, the courts have encountered a conceptual difficulty in balancing the "fiduciary" duty of authority to its ratepayers against its wide discretionary power to provide reasonable salaries and wages to its own employees and reasonable services and facilities to members of the public. In the G.L.C. *Fares Fair* case,[72] the House of Lords struck down the authority's hasty and considerable cuts in transport fares for a number of reasons, most of them grounded in the wording of the statute in question. The authority's fiduciary duty to its ratepayers was sometimes expressed as if it were a procedural duty (to take into account their interests) and at other times a substantive duty (expressed by Lord Diplock as a duty not to be "thriftless" in the use of ratepayers' money). Underlying the fiduciary duty there is surely hidden a notion of proportionality— requiring a rational balancing of the benefits to transport users against the burdens to the ratepayers.

In cases where local authority tenants have challenged rent increases as "unreasonable," the courts have also in effect applied a test of proportionality. As Diplock L.J. said in *Luby* v. *Newcastle-under-Lyme Corp*[73]:

> "the choice of rent structure involves weighing the interests of tenants as a whole and of impoverished tenants against those of the general body of ratepayers."

Town and Country Planning legislation confers discretion upon local authorities or the minister to attach conditions to the grant of a planning permission as they "think fit."[74] Despite the apparent breadth of this power, the courts have had little difficulty confining its exercise within proper limits, by insisting that the conditions are not "unreasonable" and keep within the four corners of legitimate planning goals.[75] They have had more difficulty, however, in dealing with conditions which, while not manifestly "unreasonable," in the sense used in the *Wednesbury*[76] case, and while pursuing legitimate planning goals, nevertheless derogate from the planning permission to an extent that is not acceptable.

In *Newbury District Council* v. *Secretary of State for the Environment*,[77] for example, planning permission was obtained for the change of use of an aircraft hangar to use for storage purposes. A condition attached to the permission required the building to be demolished before a given date. The House of Lords recognised that the condition furthered a proper planning purpose (to rid the area of unsightly buildings), and did not consider the condition to have been "unreasonable" in the *Wednesbury* sense. The Lords nevertheless held that the condition failed "fairly and reasonably to relate" to the permitted development. That expression is not contained in the statute itself,[78] and the Lords provided no further explanation about the relationship between the condition and the permitted development. In essence the reason for striking down the condition—although not expressly stated—was that the severity of the condition, requiring the demolition of the building itself, was out of proportion to the permission sought—which was only for a change of use and not for any "building operation."[79]

Proportionality has been used as a test of the validity not only of planning conditions but also of the refusal of a planning permission. In *Niarchos Ltd.* v. *Secretary of State for the Environment*,[80] Westminster Council refused to grant office permission in an area of London's Mayfair designated for residential use. The applicant company, which was in possession of a temporary planning permission for office use which was about to expire, appealed against the refusal. After a public enquiry, the Inspector advised the Secretary of State to grant the office permission. The Inspector took into account in his recommendation the fact that the cost of conversion of the premises to residential use would be in excess of the capital value of the premises, and would thus cause the appellant company undue hardship. The Secretary of State considered the financial hardship to the appellant to be an irrelevant consideration which he refused to take into account and thus upheld the Council's decision to refuse the permission. On appeal, the High Court held, however, that the cost of the conversion was indeed relevant, and that it was unreasonable for the Secretary of State to require the implementation of a policy

that would be "unreasonably burdensome" on the applicant.[81]
The exercise of a discretionary power (to grant or refuse planning
permission) was thus rendered *ultra vires* because of the disproportionate burden that would have been inflicted upon the company
in the implementation of a legitimate policy.

Planning condition cases also raise the point of what Professor
Wade calls "overlapping powers"[82]—an element—as we have seen
above—in the German concept of "necessity" or the American
"less restrictive alternative," which require public authorities to
employ the means that are the least harsh if more than one means
is available. In *Hall* v. *Shoreham-by-Sea U.D.C.*[83] a condition
attached to a planning permission required the developer in effect
to construct an access road to be open to the public. The High
Court struck down the condition as unreasonable, giving a clear
indication that the council ought to have adopted an alternative
course of action, namely acquiring the land from the developer
and constructing the road themselves. This alternative would have
been less harsh on the developer who would then have received
compensation for the acquisition of his land.[84] In *Royco Homes
Ltd.* v. *Hillingdom L.B.C.*[85] the Divisional Court similarly held
unlawful a planning condition that, in effect, required the
developer to provide housing to local authority standards and rent,
and to take tenants from the local authority's housing waiting list.
Apart from the conditions being "unreasonable" it was considered
that the council could not use their planning powers in this case to
achieve an objective which could, with less adverse consequence
to the developer, be achieved by alternative powers under the
Housing Acts. As Lord Justice Bridge (as he then was) said:

> "It is difficult to see how any authority could go further
> towards unburdening themselves and placing on the shoulders
> of the applicant the duty to provide housing accommodation
> which Parliament has said in Part V of the Housing Act 1957
> shall be performed by the local authority in the various ways
> in which it can be performed under that part of that Act, all of
> them requiring acquisition of the land by the local
> authority."[86]

We have seen that French law has adopted the notion of le bilan
coût-avantages (cost-benefit analysis), requiring public authorities
to balance costs and benefits of proposed projects or programmes.
Do the English courts follow a similar course?

In certain non-judicial decision-making the procedure itself is
designed to test the weight of competing notions of the public

interest. The Alkali Inspectorate, for example, enforces air pollution legislation not strictly but in a way that attempts to achieve the 'best practicable means' to eliminate pollution.[87] The law thus seeks explicitly to balance the costs of providing clean air to the owner of the works against the benefit to the public. Public inquiries into planning, transportation or power issues are further instances here.[88] If the balance of costs and benefit are not properly weighed—or seen to be weighed—by the inspector of a public inquiry or by the minister receiving his report and recommendations, will the courts, like the French courts, interfere?

Our courts do not readily interfere in the weighing of factual evidence and are even less keen to dabble in the assessment of policy alternatives. Unlike the United States, we do not have a requirement that the conclusions of administrative bodies are supported by the 'substantial evidence' in the record of a hearing.[89] Yet our law increasingly accepts that at least *some* evidence must be supplied to support a given decision. As Professor Wade says:

"To find facts without evidence is itself an abuse of power and a source of injustice, and it [the some evidence rule] ought to be within the scope of judicial review."[90]

English courts also increasingly insist that significant evidence that has been presented at a public inquiry must be adequately brought to the attention of the minister by the Inspector and that such evidence (or indeed argument) cannot be dismissed out of hand without some reason being given.[91]

Our courts may be more cautious than French Courts in substituting their view of the balance of costs and benefits for those of the relevant authority. They do however go some way to ensure that the balancing exercise is properly performed—or seen to be performed—at least to the extent of requiring some evidence to support a decision and some reasons to support the rejection of a substantial argument.

The cost-benefit notion has recently been imported into a decision whether a prisoner appearing before a board of visitors on a disciplinary charge is entitled to legal representation. The prevailing judicial view is that imprisonment by itself does not remove the right to representation. Yet the board has discretion to refuse representation. In the recent case of *Tarrant*,[92] Mr. Justice Webster listed considerations which every board ought to take into account when exercising its discretion. These include the seriousness of the charge and the potential penalty, the complexity of the case, the capacity of the prisoner, the need for despatch, and the need for fairness as between prisoners and between prisoners and prison officers. The effect of this approach is that a prisoner may only be deprived of his right to representation after a careful balancing of the costs and benefits of such a deprivation in the light of relevant considerations.[93]

This section has dealt largely with cases involving the State or a public authority as a party. However, proportionality is not only a "public law" concept. It is a general principle of law, applicable to cases that contain both "public" and "private" elements.

For example, in *International Drilling Fluids Ltd.* v. *Louisville Investments (Uxbridge) Ltd.*,[94] Lord Justice Balcombe said (in considering whether the landlord's consent to the assignment of a lease had been unreasonably withheld):

> "in my judgment the gross unfairness to the tenants of the example postulated by the judge strengthens the arguments in favour, in an appropriate case, of which the instant case is one, of it being unreasonable for the landlord not to consider the detriment to the tenant if consent is refused, where the detriment is extreme and disproportionate to the benefit to the landlord."[95]

In *Jenkins* v. *Kingsgate (Clothing Productions) Ltd.*[96] a claim of sex discrimination was upheld by the Employment Appeal Tribunal. Even though the employer in that case could show that he was pursuing a legitimate aim (*i.e.* an aim other than sex discrimination), it was held that he must also show the difference in treatment was reasonably necessary to achieve that aim; in other words (although not expressly said) proportionate to that aim.

The test of the validity of a contract in restraint of trade is in essence one of proportionality. In *Herbert Morris* v. *Saxelby*[97] the House of Lords held that, to be valid, a covenant in restraint of trade must be reasonable both in the interest of the contracting parties and in the public interest. Lord Parker of Waddington rejected the notion that the adequacy of the consideration to the covenantor was relevant to the validity of the covenant, and said

> "for a restraint to be reasonable in the interests of the parties it must afford *no more than* adequate protection to the party in whose favour it is imposed."[98]

Mr. Justice Millett in *Allied Dunbar (Frank Weisinger) Ltd.* v. *Frank Weisinger*[99] rejected the notion of proportionality as a principle by which to test the reasonableness of the restraint, apparently on the ground that there was "no objective standard" by which to weigh the detriment to the defendant against the benefits to the plaintiff, and the matter should therefore be "resolved by negotiation." However, we submit that proportionality is an appropriate test, involving, as Lord Parker put it, a consideration whether the "restraint to which he (the covenantor) subjects himself is no wider than is required for the adequate protection of the person in whose favour it is created."[1] In other words, that it is not out of proportion to the protection warranted in the circumstances.

In the different context of restraints on the public disclosure of government information, Lord Widgery C.J. stated in *Attorney General* v. *Jonathan Cape Ltd.*[2] that it is

"necessary that the restrictions imposed by the Court should not go beyond the strict requirements of the interest which it is sought to safeguard."

VII. *Conclusion*

As it has developed in European law and as it has been applied in English law, proportionality is a principle that requires a reasonable relation between a decision, its objectives and the circumstances of a given case. It requires the pursuit of legitimate ends by means that are not oppressively excessive. It looks therefore largely to the substance of decisions rather than the way they are reached, but it also requires the decision-maker not manifestly to ignore significant alternatives or interests.

We have seen that proportionality is a principle governing the exercise of discretionary powers in European Community law (which we are bound ourselves to apply). We have seen too that its underlying rationale accords with traditional English legal values. Would its explicit recognition now benefit our administrative law?

To answer that question we must first ask whether it is desirable to be explicit about the principles upon which courts review administrative action. Some would argue that it is preferable for the courts to hide their true reasons for review in the shadow of *Wednesbury* unreasonableness. We do not share that view. It seems clear to us that the legitimacy and integrity of the judicial process is in the long run damaged by vague and obscure reasoning. *Wednesbury* camouflage at best invites attack on the ground of inadequate justification and at worst invites suspicion on the ground of political motivation. Judges should mean what they say, and say what they mean.

A second question is whether proportionality is, under Lord Diplock's categories, a fourth ground of review from "irrationality," or whether it is a principle by which rationality (or reasonableness) may be tested. We have recently argued[3] that the *Wednesbury* test should now be replaced by independent principles of substantive review, of which proportionality is one.[4] Whether or not this argument is accepted, we agree with Lord Justice Woolf, who recently said that

> "Where the response is out of proportion with the cause—this provides a very clear indication of unreasonableness in a Wednesbury sense."[5]

Turning to the substance of proportionality, is it a fair and useful principle of justice in itself, or is it, as Mr. Justice Millett put it, "dangerous?"[6] In answering this question we should stress that we do not see proportionality as permitting intervention in the merits of the decisions of public officials to an extent greater than the *Wednesbury* test already allows. Like the *Wednesbury* test, proportionality is designed to guide the exercise of discretionary powers, and allows the courts to interfere with the substance of official decisions as well as the procedures by which they are reached. However it by no means releases judges from their proper reserve in interfering with decisions on the ground of policy, or assessment of fact or merits. Indeed, because proportionality advances a relatively specific legal principle—one that is at any rate far more specific than "unreasonableness" or "irrationality"—it focuses more clearly than those vaguer standards on the precise conduct it seeks to prevent. By concentrating on the specific it is more effective in excluding general considerations based on policy rather than principle.

The use of proportionality under so many different labels and in so many different contexts in English law demonstrates its general acceptance as a general principle of law. Like all grounds of judicial review it cannot be mechanically applied. Its application requires judgment in the light of the circumstances of the particular case. However, its application would affirm an important principle of justice by which all administrative action should be expected to be judged: that the decision-maker must exercise a proper sense of proportion in making a decision, and that individuals affected by decisions should not be required to bear a burden that is unnecessary or disproportionate to the ends being pursued.

Notes

[1] *Council of Civil Service Unions* v. *Minister of State for the Civil Service* [1985] A.C. 374 (HL).

[2] The grounds are legality, procedural propriety and rationality.

[3] *R.* v. *Goldsmith* [1983] 1 W.L.R. 151, at 155.

[4] In *Allied Dunbar (Frank Weisinger) Ltd.* v. *Frank Weisinger, The Times,* November 17, 1987, p. 44.

[5] *R.* v. *Secretary of State for Transport, ex p. Pegasus Holidays (London) Ltd. and Airbro (U.K.) Ltd.,* Q.B.D. August 7, 1987, Transcript CO/1377/87.

[6] Literally: relativity.

[7] See M.P. Singh, *German Administrative Law: A Common Lawyer's View* (1985), pp. 88–101.

[8] Two particular articles of the German *Grundgesetz* (Basic Law) are commonly cited as authority for the principle of *Verhältnismässigkeit*, Article 2(1) (the right of liberty) and Article 14 (the right of property).

[9] Decision of May 5, 1908, 52 PrOVG 419.

[10] Decision of November 5, 1968, 31 BVerwGE 15.

[11] Decision of October 30, 1970, 27 OVG Luneburg E321.

[12] See Tribe, *American Constitutional Law* (1978), at pp. 341–42. Professor Charles L. Black has argued expressly that the principle of proportionality applies to the interpretation of the American Bill of Rights: see "On Reading and Using the Ninth Amendment," in *The Humane Imagination* (1986), at pp. 196–97.

[13] Decision of March 16, 1907, 17 BWVGHE 227.

[14] Decision of September 29, 1965, [1966] DOV 249 (BVerwG).

[15] Decision of March 20, 1970, 22 VR 64 [BVerwG]. The freedom to pursue a vocation of one's choice is guaranteed in Article 12(1) of the Grundgesetz.

[16] 60 BVerwGE 75.

[17] Decisions of November 13, 1979, 59 BVerwGE 105 and 112.

[18] 60 BVerwGE 75, at 77.

[19] See Singh, *supra,* at 91.

[20] G. Braibant, "Le Principe de Proportionnalité," *Mélanges Walines* (1974), vol. 2, p. 297. See also his *Le droit administratif français* (1984).

[21] *Ibid.* p. 298–99. Authors' translation.

[22] See, e.g. C.E. Decembre 8, 1972, *Ville de Dieppe,* Rec 794.

[23] C.E. Fèvrier 15, 1974, *Ministre du développement industriel et scientifique* c./ Arnaud, Rec. 115.

[24] e.g. in C.E. Novembre 16, 1962, *Syndicat intercommunal d'électricité de la Nievre et autres,* Rec 612.

[25] Octobre 26, 1973, *Grassin*; Concl. A. Bernard *A.J.D.A.* 1974, 34, note J.K.

[26] *Lebon,* June 9, 1978; *A.J.D.A.* 1978, 530 Conclusions Genevois; *D.* 1979, 30 note Pacteau; *R.D.P.* 1979, 227, note Auby; *R.A.* 1978, 634, note Moderne. This case-law reverses the former, *see* Novembre 22, 1967, *Administration générale de l'assistance publique. c./Delle Chevreau, D.* 1969, 52, note Nourgeon; *Droit ouvrier,*

1968, 113 Concl. Kahn. For an example of a decision quashing an excessive sanction see July 8, 1978, Vinolay; *J.C.P.* 1980. 11. 19625, note Thouroude.

[27] See generally, L. Neville Brown and J.F. Garner, *French Administrative Law* (1983), pp. 153–161; J. Bell, "The Expansion of Judicial Review over Discretionary Powers in France," (1986), *P.L.* 99, at 113–116.

[28] *Ministre de l'équipement et du logement contre Fédération de défense des personnes concernées par le projet actuellement denommé Ville Nouvelle Est.* C.E. Mai 28, 1971. Rec. 410, Concl. Braibant.

[29] See J. Lemasurier, "Vers un nouveau principe general du droit? Le principe 'Bilan coût-avantages'," Mélanges Walines (1974) vol. 2, 551.

[30] *Supra*, note 28.

[31] C.E. Juillet 18, 1973, *Ville de Limoges.* Rec 530; *D* 1975, 49, note Collignon.

[32] C.E. Octobre 20, 1972, *Societé Civile Sainte-Marie de l'Assumption*, Rec 657, Concl. Morisot; R.D.P., 1973, 843.

[33] D. Wyatt and A. Dashwood, *The Substantive Law of the EEC* (1980).

[34] See A. Mackenzie-Stuart, "The Court of Justice of the European Communities and the Control of Executive Discretion" (1974–5) J. of S.P.T.L., p. 16, esp. 22–5; "Control of Power within the European Communities," The Holdsworth Club of Birmingham (1986); C. Schmitthoff, "The Doctrines of Proportionality and Discrimination," (1977) Eur L. Rev p. 329.

[35] *Internationale Handelsgesellschaft* v. *Einfuhr und Vorratstelle für Getreide und Futtermittel* case 11/70 [1970] E.C.R. 1125; [1972] C.M.L.R. 255.

[36] Case 36/75 [1975] E.C.R. 1219; [1976] 1 C.M.L.R. 140.

[37] Case 114/76 [1977] E.C.R. 1211. See F. Snyder, *The Law of the Common Agricultrual Policy* (1985) at 39, 56–60, 143–153.

[38] O.J. 1976 L67/18.

[39] Case 104/75 [1976] E.C.R. 613; [1976] C.M.L.R. 271. See also *Commission of the European Communities* v. *U.K., The Times*, November 6, 1988.

[40] Case 222/84 [1987] E.C.R. 83.

[41] Paragraph 38, pp. 104H–05A.

[42] Case 170/84.

[43] paragraph 37, p. 126G.

[44] [1987] I.C.R. 110 (H.L.), at 142H–43H.

[45] See J. T. Lang, "The Duties of National Courts under the Constitutional Law of the European Community," University of Exeter (1987).

[46] Convention for the Protection of Human Rights and Fundamental Freedoms, Rome, November 4, 1950; T.S. 71 (1953); Cmd 8969.

[47] *The Sunday Times case*, E.C.H.R. Judgment of April 26, 1979, Series A No. 30.

[48] Paragraph 67, p. 42.

[49] *The Case of Lithgow and others*, E.C.H.R., Judgment of May 22, 1984, Series A, No. 102.

[50] Paragraph 120, p. 50.

[51] *Sporrong and Lonroth.* Judgment of September 23, 1982, Series A, No. 52.

[52] *Lithgow. op cit.* paragraph 120, p. 50.

[53] *Ibid.*

[54] *Ibid.*

[55] " . . . typically, English law fastens, not upon principles, but upon remedies," *per* Lord Wilberforce in *Davy* v. *Spelthorne B.C.* [1984] A.C. 262 (H.L.) at 276.

[56] See Ormrod L.J.'s comments in *Northwest Holst Ltd.* v. *Secretary of State*

for Trade [1978] Ch. 201 (C.A.) at 226.

[57] See P. S. Atiyah, *Pragmatism and Theory in English Law* (1987).

[58] I Will. and Mary Sep. 2 Ch. 2.

[59] *R. v. Secretary of State for the Home Department, ex p. Herbage* (No 2) [1987] Q.B. 1077.

[60] See generally, David Thomas, *Current Sentencing Practice* (1982), A7.

[61] [1976] 1 W.L.R. 1052 (C.A.).

[62] *Ibid.* at p. 1057H.

[63] [1984] 1 C.R. 723.

[64] At p. 736H.

[65] [1985] A.C. 1054 (C.A.).

[66] [1976] 1 Q.B. 629 (C.A.). See also *R. v. London Borough of Lewisham, ex p. Shell U.K. Ltd.*, [1988] 1 All E.R. 938; 151 L.G.R. 664. (apartheid boycott beyond Council's legal powers).

[67] *R. v. London Borough of Brent, ex p. Assegai, The Times*, June 18, 1987.

[68] See J. M. Evans, *Immigration Law*, (1983), Ch. 5.

[69] *R. v. Nazari* [1980] 1 W.L.R. 1366 (C.A.).

[70] *Williams* v. *Giddy* [1911] A.C. 381 (P.C.).

[71] *The Times*, October 14, 1972

[72] *London Borough of Bromley* v. *G.L.C.* [1983] 1 A.C. 768 (H.L.).

[73] [1974] 3 All E.R. 169 (C.A.). In the recent case of *Wandsworth L.B.C.* v. *Winder* (1987) N.L.J. 124, Mervyn Davies J. applied that test to a challenge to an increase in rents and found that "this weighing or balancing was kept well in mind."

[74] s.29(1) of the Town and Country Planning Act, 1971.

[75] See generally M. Grant, *Urban Planning Law* (1986) Ch. 8.

[76] *Associated Provincial Picture Houses Ltd.* v. *Wednesbury Corporation* [1948] 1 K.B. 223 (C.A.).

[77] [1980] A.C. 528 (H.L).

[78] It was first used by Lord Denning in *Pyx Granite Co. Ltd.* v. *Minister of Housing and Local Government* [1958] 1 Q.B. 554 (C.A.) at 572. See Grant, *supra*, at 338 *et seq.*

[79] It was however stressed by all their Lordships in *Newbury* that there may be cases when a condition containing the requirement of an operation might "fairly and reasonably" relate to a permission for a change of use.

[80] (1977) 76 L.G.R. 480 (D.C.).

[81] A policy in the local development plan was considered relevant in this case, requiring conversion to residential use if the premises were "reasonably" capable of adaption.

[82] H. W. R. Wade, *Administrative Law* (1982) (5th ed.) p. 368.

[83] [1964] 1 All E.R. 1 (D.C.).

[84] But see *Westminster Bank Ltd.* v. *M.H.L.G.* [1971] A.C. 508 (H.L.).

[85] [1974] Q.B. 720 (D.C.).

[86] *Ibid.* at 733.

[87] See Grant, *supra*, note 75, at 446.

[88] Under EEC Directive 85/337 which is to become mandatory in all Member States in June 1988, all major land-use projects will require Environmental Impact Statements, containing an analysis of the likely effects of the project on the environment and the steps the developer proposes to carry out to mitigate those effects.

[89] Administrative Procedure Act, 1946, now codified under 5 USC s.10, para. 706. See S. Breyer and R. Stewart, *Administrative Law and Regulatory Policy*, 522–524 (1979).

[90] Wade, *supra*, p. 293.

[91] See e.g. *Barnham* v. *Secretary of State for the Environment and Hertfordshire C.C.* [1985] J.P.L. p. 861.

[92] *R.* v. *Home Secretary, ex p. Tarrant* [1985] Q.B. 251 (D.C.).

[93] Compare the "balancing" required in immigration cases (*supra*, note 69) and local authority rent cases (*supra*, note 73). Webster J.'s reasoning in *Tarrant* was approved by the House of Lords in *R.* v. *Board of Visitors of H.M. Prison, the Maze, ex p. Hone* [1988] 2 W.L.R. 177.

[94] [1986] Ch. 513 (C.A.).

[95] *Ibid.* at 522.

[96] [1981] I.C.R. 715.

[97] [1916] A.C. 688 (H.L.).

[98] *Ibid.* at 706.

[99] *The Times*, November 17, 1987.

[1] *Ibid.* note 96 at 707.

[2] [1976] 2 Q.B. 752 (D.C.) at 771A. See also *Attorney General* v. *Guardian Newspapers Ltd. and others* [the "Spycatcher" case] [1987] 3 All E.R. 316, where Lord Templeman (at 355), with whom Lord Ackner agreed (at 364), adopted the test under the European Human Rights Convention as applied in the *Sunday Times* case (*supra*, note 47) which requires interference with freedom of expression not to exceed that which is "necessary in a democratic society." At the trial Scott J. held that the claim for an injunction against *The Observer* and *The Guardian* in June 1986 was not "proportionate to the legitimate aim pursued" (at p. 88 of the transcript). At the date of writing that judgment is subject to a pending appeal. It is noteworthy that as long ago as 1952 the Supreme Court of India explained (when interpreting an exception to the constitutional guarantee of freedom of association permitting "reasonable" restrictions) that "the disproportion of the imposition" should be one of a number of factors taken into account. *State of Madras* v. *V.G. Row* (1952) S.C.R. 597 *per* Sastri C.J.

[3] J. Jowell and A. Lester "Beyond Wednesbury: Substantive Principles of Administrative Law," *Public Law*, Autumn 1987, p. 368.

[4] Kennedy J. recently, and, in our view, correctly, referred to the "administrative law concepts of reasonableness and proportionality" (*R.* v. *Home Secretary, ex p. Read* [1988] 1 All E.R. 759 (D.C.), p. 767 f), apparently reflecting Lord Diplock's view that proportionality is a separate ground of review from rationality.

[5] In *R.* v. *Brent L.B.C., ex p. Assegai, supra,* note 67.

[6] In *Allied Dunbar, supra,* note 98.

The Courts and the Policy Making Process

DAWN OLIVER

I. *Introduction*

At first sight it may appear inappropriate in a book of essays on new directions in administrative law to devote a chapter to the subject of the courts and the policy-making process. In the light of House of Lords' decisions *In re Findlay*[1] on parole policy and *Bushell* v. *Secretary of State for the Environment*[2] on public inquiries into highway policy, it might be inferred that the jurisdiction of the courts in judicial review does not extend to the policy-making process. However, it will be argued in this chapter that there is ample authority for the proposition that the courts are willing in principle to review the policy process and that cases in which review has been refused may be seen as exceptions to a general rule that policy-makers must adopt fair and open procedures.

There is an extensive literature in the fields of public administration and political theory on the policy-making process. The central concern of this writing tends towards the effectiveness of policy-making and implementation. By contrast public lawyers generally concentrate on legal and constitutional proprieties and the protection of individuals and society against unfairness or abuse of power by state institutions. This difference of emphasis reflects the unavoidable conflict generated by the twin requirements that government should be in a position to get on with the job of governing, and at the same time that it should be subject to checks and balances and the rule of law. Recently Sir Douglas Wass has complained about the inadequacy of existing, largely non-legal, institutional safeguards against arbitrary and inefficient policy-making by government,[3] and he has proposed a number of reforms in order to improve the policy process. These include a Freedom of Information Act, additional support for the opposition, improved parliamentary procedures, the setting up of Specialist Consultative Bodies, and a Standing Commission on Public Policy. Against this background of concern to improve the policy-making process, the subject of inquiry in this paper is the extent to which the courts also have a role in supervising the policy-making process.

A problem in attempting to write about law and policy is the ambiguity of the latter term. The definition of policy proposed by Friend *et al* as "essentially a stance which, once articulated, contributes to the context within which a succession of future decisions will be made"[4] is helpful for present purposes in emphasising the distinction between a decision or an action, and a policy that influences a decision or action. An important difference is that decisions and actions may directly affect individual or private rights, duties and interests, whereas a policy only does so indirectly: a policy only affects particular interests when a decision is taken to implement it. Although the distinction between policy and decision is not always clear cut it is one that will be pursued in this article as far as possible in order to avoid discussion of questions such as whether an exception should be made to a given policy; instead the question for consideration will be whether the policy itself, that lies behind a decision, may be challenged, for example because of some defect in the policy-making process, or new evidence that undermines the policy.

II. *Judicial Requirements of the Policy-Making Process*

The courts have fairly consistently indicated that policies should be carefully formulated and reviewed from time to time, particularly if new data or experience suggest that a reappraisal is required. In *Franklin* v. *Minister of Housing and Local Government*[5] the House of Lords held that the Minister's strongly held policy on new towns, and particularly on Stevenage, had not in fact fettered his discretion. But it is noteworthy that in reaching the conclusion that the Minister's decision should stand Lord Thankerton for one was influenced by the fact that before making the draft order the Minister must have made inquiries and had consultations.[6] In this comment Lord Thankerton indicates that the policy-making process might enter into the sum as a consideration where, as in this case, a policy containing a mixture of ideological elements, party political issues, interference with rights and a factual basis is in issue.

More recently in *Nottinghamshire County Council* v. *Secretary of State for the Environment*[7] Lord Templeman was influenced in his decision not to review guidance issued by the Secretary of State by the fact that

> "The principles inspiring the 1985–86 guidance were carefully considered and evolved in the light of experience and with the obvious desire to carry out in an even-handed and equitable manner fair to all local authorities the task imposed on the Minister in the national interest of securing overall economies."[8]

In the light of these comments it is emphasised at this point that the cases about judicial review of the policy-making process that are discussed in this chapter concern policies made by Ministers, councillors, officials, chief constables; and high-level policy decisions as well as operational policies. It will be seen that there is no general rule that the policy-making process adopted by politicians is immune from supervision by the courts.

A duty to review policy?

Most areas of state activity are covered by existing policies, even if the policy is one of non-intervention. A question that arises from time to time is whether existing policy should be reviewed in the light of new evidence about its effectiveness or appropriateness. In principle the courts have accepted such a duty.

In *British Oxygen Corporation* v. *The Ministry of Technology*[9] the main issue was the application of a policy rather than its merits or how it had been formulated. However, Lord Reid expressed the view that

> "There may be cases where an officer or authority ought to listen to a substantial argument reasonably presented urging a change of policy."[10]

The policy at issue in *British Oxygen* had been expressed in the form of administrative rules, and was of an operational kind made for reasons of administrative convenience and expediency and contained little in the way of ideological or party political content. It is difficult to see why any policy-maker should refuse to listen to argument of this kind unless, perhaps, there is a high value content in the policy (see later).

In the Toxteth policing case, *R.* v. *Oxford, ex p. Levey*[11] the Court of Appeal indicated that a policy-maker ought in principle to be prepared to review his policy in the light of experience, and found for the Chief Constable partly because he had reviewed his policing policy. The Master of the Rolls stated in *Levey* that while

> "Chief Constables have the widest possible discretion in their choice of methods to discharge their duty (to keep the peace and enforce the law)... Any officer who found that his chosen methods were ineffective would be under a duty to re-examine them and consider what alteration was required, but one incident, or even several, would not be a sound basis for such a re-examination or, a fortiori, a change."[12]

The implication of this comment would appear to be that a court might be willing to grant mandamus to require a chief constable to review a policy if he found it to be ineffective. Presumably if it could be established (which is unlikely) that a public authority had found its policy to be ineffective the courts would be willing to require a policy review if the authority failed to conduct one.

The factual basis of policy

A question that arises from time to time is whether a policy-maker must establish a factual foundation for his policy, or whether he may proceed on the basis of assumptions that a factual basis exists. In *Sagnata Investments* v. *Norwich Corporation*[13] the Recorder had allowed the applicants' appeal on the ground that the Council had no evidence to support its belief that amusement arcades would be harmful to young people. This approach was followed by the Court of Appeal where the question was asked, in effect "how can a local authority claim to have considered the merits of a case if it acts on a policy for which there is no evidence?"[14]

Galligan[15] has made the point in relation to *Sagnata* that policies cannot always be based on facts, or only on facts, because matters of judgment enter into the picture: "a policy represents a choice of social goals and values for which reasons may be given, but which cannot be reduced to questions of fact for objective determination."[16]

However there will be policies where a mixture of fact and value judgment combine to produce the policy. It is suggested that in those cases there should be some procedure for testing the factual basis in order to establish the rationality of the policy. *Sagnata* may be taken as an indication that in those cases where a factual basis for a policy is required, the courts will intervene to discover whether the basis exists, or whether evidence had been made available to the policy-maker in formulating the policy. *Sagnata* also indicates, it is suggested, that the courts may get it wrong, by leaving too little space for value judgments. If the facts are self-evident and relatively unimportant when weighed against the element of value judgment in the policy, the courts should hesitate to intervene.

Policy affecting rights and expectations

Some policies affect the rights, interests and legitimate expectations of individuals or corporate bodies: policies on land use planning affect the rights of land-owners; and policies on immigration (*R.* v. *Home Secretary, ex p. Asif Khan*[17]), parole (*In re Findlay*[18]) and rate support grant (*Brent*[19]) affect the interests or expectations of immigrants, prisoners and local authorities respectively.

Generally where *rights* are directly affected by a policy there are statutory procedures (e.g. public inquiries) for safeguarding those rights before a binding decision is taken to implement the policy. By contrast there are few statutory provisions protecting *interests* or legitimate expectations from policy changes. However there is some authority to support the view that the courts will step in to control the procedures for changing policy by requiring that changes affecting legitimate expectations ought to be preceded by publicity, warning or consultation. These processes serve to secure the consent or acquiescence of affected groups, inform the policy-maker in advance of any logical or other weaknesses in the policy, and avoid problems about the legitimacy of the change of policy.[20]

In *R.* v. *Secretary of State for the Environment, ex p. Brent London Borough Council*[21] the council's expectation of rate support grant was in issue. The question was whether the Secretary of State should have been prepared to listen to arguments in favour of a change of policy. The Queen's Bench Division held that where the Secretary of State refused to listen to representations urging him to change his policy he was unlawfully fettering his discretion.

> "His attitude was in effect that the policy was settled...the Secretary of State clearly decided to turn a deaf ear to any and all representations to change the policy formulated by him before he obtained his statutory powers."[22]

This passage echoes the view of Lord Reid in *British Oxygen* quoted above.

Value judgments in policy: The Findlay case

As has been seen problems arise where there is a conflict between
the desire of a policy-maker to follow his own value judgments,
and the need to establish a factual basis, or to give special
consideration to those whose rights, interests or legitimate
expectations are affected by policy. The *Brent* case indicates that a
willingness on the part of a policy-maker to reopen a policy
may be required, *inter alia*, where rights or legitimate expectations
are affected, even if the policy itself is at a fairly high level, forms
part of a broad government strategy and involves a high degree
of value judgment. On this point the *Brent* case appears to be
inconsistent with the approach in the case on parole policy, *In
re Findlay.*[23]

This case raised issues about whether consultations should take
place prior to changes in policy that both affect legitimate
expectations and involve politically sensitive value judgments. The
Home Secretary had altered his policy on the granting of parole to
certain classes of prisoner without any prior consultation with the
parole board, or any of the prisoners' pressure groups. The Home
Secretary did however consult the parole board on the precise way
in which his policy, once formulated, should be achieved. There
was therefore two levels of policy in the *Findlay* case, the "high
level" policy on parole and the lower level "operational" policy on
the process by which the former could be achieved.

In upholding the Home Secretary's omission to consult the
parole board in formulating the high level policy Lord Scarman
focussed on the politically sensitive nature of the policy. The
Home Secretary was, he said, entitled, in making the policy, to
take into account matters such as "public confidence in our
criminal justice system"[24] and "public concern about violent
crime."[25] "Neither the board nor the judiciary can be as close or as
sensitive to public opinion as a minister responsible to Parliament
and to the electorate."[26] "He has to judge the public acceptability
of early release and to determine the policies needed to maintain
public confidence in the system of criminal justice."[27] Matters of
this kind were " . . . plainly material matters for his consideration
in the exercise of his discretion. He cannot therefore be said to
have acted unreasonably in having regard to them."[28]

It is difficult to see how the fact that these matters *are relevant*
leads to the conclusion that *therefore* there was no duty to consult
the parole board. The assumption seems to have been that parole
policy is *only* about inherently political value judgments; or that
policy at a high level is inherently non-justiciable or unreopenable;

or that no process should be imposed on a policy-maker operating at a high or controversial level.

None of these assumptions is supported by other cases. Compare, for instance, the *Brent*[29] case, where the court imposed a duty to consult and to be ready to reconsider a policy about the level of rate support grant awarded to local authorities, despite the fact that the policy in question was highly political and made at a high level in government; and *Bromley* v. *G.L.C.*[30] where the House of Lords objected to the fact that the Labour Council, once elected, had not carefully reconsidered the policy they had proposed in their manifesto, and which was, again, highly political and value-laden; and the *G.C.H.Q.* case,[31] where it was held that a politically very sensitive decision made by the Prime Minister (what could be a higher level than that?) should in principle have been preceded by consultation but for the national security issue.

The policy change in *Findlay* affected the legitimate expectations of individuals, and as has been suggested this consideration indicates a need either to consult some representative body (although the parole board does not represent prisoners); or to adopt a cautious and open approach to changing policy in order to legitimate the change; or to defer change in order not to disappoint legitimate expectations (compare the *Asif Khan*[32] and *Ruddock*[33] cases, below). The absence of any recognised body representing prisoners may have been crucial in the *Findlay* case. If one had existed, it is suggested, the House of Lords may well have found a duty to consult, in line with the decision in the *G.C.H.Q.* case. If such a body had been available and consultation had taken place, it would not have prevented the Secretary of State from giving such weight as he wished to the matters set out above, and reaching the same conclusion. But the process would have gained in rationality and legitimacy.[34]

However, given Lord Scarman's emphasis on the political judgments involved in the parole policy, the case may be taken to decide that where a policy consists solely of value-judgments and does not contain any questionable factual assumptions, consultation is not necessary. On that basis the decision would be unobjectionable. If, however, it is taken to indicate that there is no duty to consult where some representative organisation or pressure group is available and where legitimate expectations, either of consultation, or of substantive benefits, are affected, that would appear to be contrary to the principles formulated in the cases referred to earlier.

Openness

A policy-maker may choose of his own volition to adopt an
open but informal procedure, and the courts have on occasions
approved this approach. In the lorry ban case *R.* v. *Secretary
of State for Transport, ex p. Greater London Council*[35] the
Court of Appeal attached importance to the fact that the
G.L.C. had set up a panel of inquiry to examine the social,
economic and environmental effects of banning lorries from
the Greater London Area before making the order. The court
upheld the G.L.C. decision not to hold a public inquiry before
making a draft "lorry ban" order. This may be taken to imply
that informal administrative processes of consultation are more
appropriate than, for example, formal public inquiries for many
policy issues, and the courts will approve such processes.

Departures from Guidelines

There have been cases where an existing policy has been published in the form of quasi-legislative rules such as guidelines.
Turpin has commented that "quasi-legislative rules are a means
by which the administration injects specific policies into the
exercise of its discretionary powers."[36] It is well established
that these guidelines should not be so rigidly applied as to
preclude a potential beneficiary of a discretionary power from
all hope of consideration.[37] It has recently been held that
guidelines can give rise to a legitimate expectation that they
will be applied and will not be altered or departed from to the
detriment of particular individuals without republication.

In *Asif Khan*[38] for example the Home Secretary had issued a
circular stating his policy on the admission of children from
overseas for adoption. This had raised a legitimate expectation
on the part of would-be adopters of a child from Pakistan that
he would be permitted to enter the country; it was held that
the Home Secretary could not then refuse entry on the basis of
some other, unpublished, criterion. He could not, without
warning or consultation, put into effect an alteration to his
policy.

The policy issue in *Asif Khan* was not one involving ideology
or high level government policy. There is no real problem of
large numbers of children from abroad being adopted to evade
the immigration laws. If there had been it is doubtful whether
the court would have so fettered the minister in his power to
alter policy. The *Findlay* approach might have been adopted.

In another case on departure from guidelines, *R.* v. *Secretary of State for the Home Dept., ex p. Ruddock*,[39] it was held that the Secretary of State was bound by a duty of fairness not to depart from the Home Office's published guidelines on the issuing of warrants for telephone tapping[40] even though the applicant might not have been aware of the terms of those guidelines. It is not easy to reconcile this approach with *Findlay*. Both cases concerned the balancing of legitimate expectations and ministerial value judgments about public opinion and the public interest. And yet in one case expectations were protected and in the other the minister's freedom to alter policy to the detriment of expectations without consultation was upheld.

Party politics in policy-making

Currently one of the most problematic aspects of the policy-making process lies in determining how much room should be allowed for party-political considerations such as tactical voting by councillors, avoiding political embarrassment, fulfilling manifesto pledges and implementing ideological preferences.

One of the best known and most controversial cases is *Bromley London Borough Council* v. *Greater London Council*[41] in which the policy of elected local government councillors fell to be considered. One of the issues was the policy-making process that had produced the "fares fair" policy. A number of the judges who heard the case took exception to the way in which the policy had been formulated before the election, and then put into effect within a matter of days of the election without consultation or reconsideration and on the basis that the manifesto bound the Labour group to implement the policy.[42] Here we have a clear indication that the courts may impose a prudent policy-making process and a duty to consult, although not laying down formal procedures to be followed.

By contrast with the *Bromley* case in *R.* v. *Merseyside County Council, ex p. Great Universal Stores Ltd.*[43] the policy on fare reductions had been put to the electorate, and after the election the Council had considered information as to the practicability of withdrawing the previously proposed reductions in services and the cost of reducing fares as outlined in the election manifesto. Woolf J. held that whether the decision was lawful or not would depend on how it was reached and, given the council's careful consideration of practicability and cost the decision was unobjectionable.[44] Woolf J. compared the *Bromley* case with the instant case and held that since in the latter case more temperate consideration was given to the desirability and consequences of putting into effect the previously announced policy it should not be challenged.[45]

In the *G. U.S.* case Woolf J. gave an indication of the procedure to be followed in policy-making. The council did not have to consider alternatives so long as, having considered a single proposal, they came to the conclusion that it was a proper proposal to adopt.[46] The burden on a policy-maker, then, in that sort of case, is not particularly onerous: he does not have to look at each and every possible alternative, but he must carefully consider the implications of the policy he prefers in principle.

Collective policy-making can raise issues about the participation in the process of persons other than those who are legally and constitutionally responsible for policy. In *Bromley* v. *G.L.C.* the House of Lords objected to the suggestion that G.L.C. councillors were mandated to pursue their manifesto policies,[47] and expressed reservations about permitting persons other than elected councillors to make policy decisions. Manifestos are drawn up by committees consisting of members of a party, not only candidates for election. Oliver L.J. in the Court of Appeal in *Bromley* v. *G.L.C.* objected that

> "We do not know who prepared the manifesto, much less do we know what information he or they had in formulating it . . . The authors of the manifesto are not the Council."[48]

Where, for example, organisations and committees within the political parties discuss and reach decisions about policy, these should not be regarded as binding on councillors if those committees or organisations were composed of members who are not councillors. In *R.* v. *Waltham Forest L.B.C., ex p. Waltham Forest Ratepayers' Action Group*[49] Sir John Donaldson, M.R. emphasised that a decision by councillors made on instructions from a body such as the Local Government Group would be invalid.[50]

Collective policy-making has become a particular problem in local government, where policy is supposedly made by "the council" but in fact by the majority party. Since judgments about politically controversial matters are unlikely to be easily reached in a committee where members of majority and minority parties operate jointly it is not surprising that councillors should have sought ways to avoid multi-party policy-making on occasions.

The problem is illustrated by the *Chadwick*[51] case; the applicant, a member of an opposition party on the Sheffield City

Council, and a member of the council's policy committee, complained that a sub-committee of the policy committee, composed solely of members of the ruling party, was receiving advice from council officers in formulating policy, and that those reports from officers were not being made available to him as a member of the policy committee. He applied for an order entitling him to see these reports. It was held that the use of a sub-committee partly for political purposes, and the consequent need for secrecy which would not otherwise have arisen, could not justify exclusion of the applicant or denying him access to reports from officers; he had established a "need to know" the content of these reports, and the council had acted unreasonably in the "Wednesbury sense" in deciding that he did not.

The difficulties in formulating policy and making political judgments in the relatively open setting of committees which include members of parties other than the ruling party or parties were put starkly by David Blunkett of Sheffield City Council in an affidavit in this case; he stated that if opposition councillors were to attend deliberative, policy-making committees, the discussion of policy would take place instead at informal meetings of councillors from which opposition members would be excluded; this would cause problems about whether officers could give their advice, and whether minutes would be kept. Woolf J expressed some sympathy with this view, though he decided the case against Sheffield on other grounds. These were that, although exclusion of an opposition member from a committee meeting of which he was not a member was not unlawful (unless Standing Orders provided otherwise) the sub-committee in this instance was exceeding the functions that had been delegated to it by the policy committee by working out a policy which a group of members of the council, rather than the council itself, wished to adopt.[52]

Another aspect of the collective decision-making process is the possibility that a policy reached in private by a group of members of one party may be influenced by improper considerations of political self-interest. In *Padfield*,[53] it will be recalled, the members of the House of Lords objected to the suggestion that policy-makers are entitled to be influenced by considerations of party political advantage to the exclusion of the public interest or the policy of the enabling Act. The Minister had refused to refer a complaint to a committee because he feared political opposition to the recommendation that the committee was likely to make, that the price of milk should be increased. Lord Upjohn was clear that "policy must not be based on political considerations which ... are pre-eminently extraneous. ... This fear of parliamentary trouble ... if an inquiry were ordered and its possible results is alone sufficient to vitiate the Minister's decision which ... can never validly turn on purely political considerations; he must be prepared to face the music in Parliament if a statute has cast upon him an obligation in the proper exercise of a discretion conferred upon him to order a reference to the committee of investigation."

Lord Reid in *Padfield* held that if the minister's view was that he was

"entitled to refuse to refer a complaint because if he did so he might later find himself in an embarrassing situation that would plainly be a bad reason."

However in the *Waltham Forest* case[54] the Court of Appeal took a more indulgent view of party political self-interest. Sir John Donaldson M.R. found that it was "a wholly tenable view that (a councillor) would serve the citizens of Waltham Forest better by voting in accordance with the wishes of the majority of the Labour group and continuing to oppose their policy on expenditure from within"[55] rather than voting in accordance with his own independent judgment of the wisdom of the proposal. Labour Party Standing Orders which required councillors to refrain from speaking or voting in opposition to decisions of the Labour group were, the Master of the Rolls found, not objectionable as long as these orders did not require a councillor to resign from the council[56]: but councillors must remember that whatever importance they attached to group unity, the ultimate decision was for them as individuals.[57]

It is clear that there is currently a problem in finding room for party political and ideological value judgments in the policy-making process. The House of Lords was hostile to "eccentric principles of socialistic philanthropy" in *Roberts* v. *Hopwood*[58] and in effect the decision struck at the roots of the council's policy on equal pay and fair wages and seemed to deny the council the right to implement party policy. A similar dislike of party policy is expressed by Lord Denning M.R. in the Court of Appeal in *Bromley* v. *G.L.C.*[59]: "when the party gets into power it should consider any proposal afresh—on its merits—without any feeling of being obliged to honour it or being committed to it."

A different and more restrained, and it is suggested more realistic, attitude to party policy was adopted by Woolf J. in *R. v. Amber Valley District Council, ex p. Jackson.*[60] Here it was alleged that Labour councillors were disqualified from dealing with a planning application because the Labour party was strongly in favour of the granting of permission. The councillors, while acknowledging that it was their policy to support the application, maintained that they would consider the application and objections fairly as they were legally obliged to do. Woolf J. refused to intervene, holding that "the department is under an obligation to be fair and carefully to consider the evidence . . . but the fact that it has a policy on the matter does not entitle a court to intervene." In the *Waltham Forest* case[61] the judges gave the councillors the benefit of any doubts about the influence of the party on the exercise of judgment by individual councillors. "The distinction between giving great weight to the views of colleagues and to party policy on the one hand, and voting blindly in support of party policy may on occasion be a fine one, but it is nevertheless very real."[62]

III. *Arguments of Expediency and Inconvenience Against the Reopening of Policy Issues*

The cases considered above have been concerned with the question whether and when a policy-maker may be regarded as bound to reconsider a policy. They indicate a willingness in principle on the part of the courts to intervene. In some cases however the courts have entertained arguments of a political or practical kind against the reopening of policy issues where the requirements of policy-making have not been met. It has been suggested, for example, that it would be inconvenient, time-consuming and expensive to reopen a policy; or that policy issues should be examined, if at all, in a formal, quasi-inquisitorial forum, and that this is not legally permissible; or conversely that policy issues are better aired informally, in an advisory committee or some similar organisation; or that it would be politically embarrassing to reopen a policy issue; or that political channels are more appropriate for securing a policy review than an indication from the court that a policy should be re-examined.

Whether administrative inconvenience justifies a refusal to permit policy to be challenged must depend on such matters as the level of the policy at issue, the forum in which it is being considered, whether some alternative and more appropriate review process is available, the circumstances of the particular case and other considerations pointing either way. In *R.* v. *Broadcasting Complaints Commission, ex p. Owen*[63] for example, David Owen sought mandamus and a declaration that the Commission should consider his complaint that the Social Democratic Party had been unfairly treated in television news programmes broadcast by the BBC and the I.B.A. He was challenging the policies on achieving political balance in broadcasting. The Queen's Bench Divisional Court expressly rejected a plea by the Commission that it was justified in refusing to consider a complaint by the fact that investigation would impose too great a burden on their limited staff,[64] although the Court rejected Dr. Owen's application on other grounds (see below).

A suitable forum for review?

Policy issues may arise that are susceptible to be reopened, but only if a suitable forum or procedure, whether formal or informal, is available. This was another of the problems in the *Broadcasting Complaints Commission*[65] case. The court expressed the view that if the Commission were to embark on the task of deciding whether the policy of the broadcasting authority was fair or unfair, there would have to be provision for hearings and participation for interested organisations, such as the other political parties.[66] The court therefore contemplated that it would at least be possible for the Commission to embark on the task if, but only if, proper hearings could be held. In this case the legislation did not permit such hearings and this led the court to uphold the Commission's refusal to consider the complaint.

There have been instances where inconvenience is accepted as a persuasive argument against reconsidering a policy, particularly if the position is that inconvenience will be caused if the matter is raised in the process to which the application relates, whereas a more appropriate forum exists in which the matter may be reviewed without inconvenience. The *Bushell*[67] case is an example of this approach.

The reasons given by the majority in the House of Lords in *Bushell* for their decision that cross-examination on the Red Book methodology of traffic forecasting need not have been permitted at a public inquiry were principally concerned with inconvenience, and the inappropriateness of the public inquiry as the forum for such investigation. Lord Lane felt that to allow cross-examination would have meant "an even lengthier hearing without any appreciable advantage"[68] because, in his view, the witness would clearly have maintained that the Red Book was the best guide available at the time! Viscount Dilhorne was of the opinion that "the views of departmental witnesses as to the comparative merits of different methods of forecasting traffic elicited in the course of cross-examination are not likely to affect the ultimate outcome."[69] The outcome of cross-examination and any recommendation based upon it was, in the view of Lord Diplock, likely to be unreliable, and thus cross-examination would have been a waste of time. This was because the inspector's consideration would be limited by the material which happened to be presented to him at the particular inquiry and "it would be a rash inspector who based on that kind of material a positive recommendation to the minister that the method of predicting traffic needs throughout the country should be changed and it would be an unwise minister who acted in reliance on it."[70]

Viscount Dilhorne in *Bushell* was influenced by the fact that there existed a Standing Committee (the Leitch Committee) which could subject the technical questions about traffic forecasting to rigorous examination; he said: "How much time was spent at this inquiry in examination of technical issues I do not know but with such issues being monitored by a standing advisory committee the case for not permitting them to be debated at a local public inquiry appears to me to be strong."[71] The matter was "fit to be debated in a wider forum"[72] and "... a local inquiry does not provide a suitable forum in which to debate what is in the relevant sense a matter of government policy.[73]

Lord Edmund-Davies disagreed with the majority in *Bushell* on all counts, except that questions relating to the merits of government policy could not be raised at a public inquiry. He treated the question of traffic "need" as being not a question of policy but of fact.[74]

Lord Edmund-Davies adopted the view of the Franks Committee. "We see no reason why the factual basis for a departmental view should not be explained and its validity tested in cross-examination"[75] This view is similar to the approach in *Sagnata*, which was discussed above: generally the courts will expect factual assumptions to be carefully explored and their basis established, unless the factual element in a policy is minimal, as in *Re Findlay* (above). Lord Edmund-Davies also disagreed with the view of the majority that it would have been a waste of time to allow cross-examination of the witnesses; and he felt that there was a duty of natural justice which could not be displaced in favour of considerations of inconvenience, over-judicialisation, saving of time, or the appropriateness of the forum. In other words rejected arguments of expediency against raising matters of fact, or mixed fact and opinion.

In the *Gwent* case[76] the treatment of policy issues at public inquiries arose again. The issue here was whether an inspector at an inquiry was obliged to make recommendations about policy issues that had been raised at the inquiry, or whether his duty was limited to reporting to the minister on the arguments that had been put forward about it. Here, as in *Bushell*, the Court of Appeal was weighing up the right of a minister to make a political decision and the inconvenience or waste of time in allowing or requiring detailed reconsideration of a policy at an inquiry or in an inspector's report, and concluded in favour of arguments of expediency and against the reopening of policy.

✕ IV. *Conclusion*

The courts have shown a willingness in recent cases to extend the frontiers of judicial review beyond decision-making and into the policy-making process. However policy is an unruly horse and the courts have not been entirely consistent in their attempts to tame it.

In the cases discussed above the courts have developed a number of principles of open-mindedness, openness, rationality, respect for rights and expectations, and constitutional propriety in the policy-making process. These do not have exact parallels in the public administration literature on the policy process. This point highlights the respective limits and the different roles of the disciplines of law and public administration. The latter discipline is concerned more with the realities of administration and its effectiveness; the law has a dual role to play; it is the instrument through which many public policies are implemented, as is illustrated by *Findlay* and *Bushell*. But it is also concerned with the protection of individuals, the control of power and the protection of established constitutional values.

The cases establish that in principle policy ought to be reconsidered if affected interests were not consulted, or the necessary factual basis (if any) for the policy does not exist, or the policy was not carefully considered, or new evidence or arguments that undermine the policy have emerged. The cases may be taken to indicate that the only acceptable reasons for a policy-maker refusing to reconsider a policy if these grounds are established by a person having a sufficient interest in the matter are that the policy is overwhelmingly a matter of value judgment, or that a suitable procedure or forum for policy review is not available. In effect the courts distinguish between principled and political considerations in deciding whether the policy-making process is reviewable. This distinction between principled and political arguments about the policy-making process and the reopening of policy is an important one, and I suggest that the reasons why courts have been reluctant to require the reopening of policy in cases such as *Findlay* and *Bushell* are generally political in this sense, and do not imply the inherent non-justiciability or unreopenability of policy.

Notes

[1] [1985] A.C. 318.
[2] [1981] A.C. 75, H.L.
[3] Sir Douglas Wass "Checks and balances in public policy making," (1987) *Public Law*, 181.
[4] J. K. Friend, J. M. Power and C. L. J. Yewlett *Public Planning: The Intercorporate Dimension*, 1974, at p. 40; for a good review of the literature on the meanings of "policy" see C. Ham and M. Hill *The Policy Process in the Modern Capitalist State*, 1984, at pp. 11–13.
[5] [1948] A.C. 87, H.L.
[6] *Ibid.* at 102. See also 98–99.
[7] [1986] A.C. 240, H.L.
[8] *Ibid.* at 267.
[9] [1971] A.C. 610, H.L.
[10] *Ibid.* at 625.
[11] *R.* v. *Oxford, ex p. Levey,* Court of Appeal, October 30, 1986.
[12] *Ibid.*
[13] [1972] 2 Q.B. 614, C.A.
[14] See Galligan "The nature and function of policies within discretionary power" (1974) *Public Law* 332, at 341.
[15] *Ibid.*
[16] *Ibid.* at 342.
[17] [1984] 1 W.L.R. 1337, C.A.
[18] [1985] A.C. 318.
[19] [1982] Q.B. 593, D.C.
[20] [1971] A.C. 610 at 625.
[21] [1982] Q.B. 593, D.C. The issue in *Brent* was not departure from the rule or policy.
[22] *Ibid.* at 644.
[23] [1985] A.C. 318.
[24] *Ibid.* at 333, 334, 335.
[25] *Ibid.* 326.
[26] *Ibid.* at 333.

²⁷ *Ibid.* at 333.
²⁸ *Ibid.* at 334.
²⁹ [1982] Q.B. 593.
³⁰ [1983] A.C. 768, H.L.
³¹ *Council of Civil Service Unions* v. *Minister for the Civil Service* [1985] A.C. 374.
³² *R.* v. *Secretary of State for the Home Department, ex p. Asif Mahmood Khan* [1984] 1 W.L.R. 1337, C.A.
³³ [1987] 1 W.L.R. 1482.
³⁴ See Comment by Genevra Richardson at (1985) *Public Law*, 34.
³⁵ [1985] Q.B. 556.
³⁶ C. Turpin *British Government and the Constitution*, 1985, pp. 325–326.
³⁷ *British Oxygen Corporation* v. *The Ministry of Technology* [1971] A.C. 610, H.L.
³⁸ *R.* v. *Secretary of State for the Home Department, ex p. Asif Mahmood Khan* [1984] 1 W.L.R. 1337, C.A.
³⁹ [1987] 2 All E.R. 518, Taylor J.
⁴⁰ The decision is still authority on the duty to follow published guidelines, although on the matter of telephone tapping the position is now governed by the Interception of Communications Act 1985.
⁴¹ [1983] A.C. 768, H.L.
⁴² *Ibid. per* Lord Diplock at 829–831; *per* Lord Brandon at 853; and in the Court of Appeal, *per* Lord Denning M.R. at 776; and Oliver L.J. at 789–90. See also *R.* v. *London Transport Executive, ex p. Greater London Council* [1983] 1 Q.B. 484, at 497, *per* Kerr L.J.
⁴³ (1982) 80 L.G.R. 639, Woolf J.
⁴⁴ *Ibid.* at 649.
⁴⁵ *Ibid.* at 651, 657.
⁴⁶ *Ibid.* at 657. Compare Lord Denning M.R. in *Bromley* v. *Greater London Council* [1982] 3 W.L.R. at 69–70. See also *Estranco Ltd.* v. *Greater London Council* [1982] 1 W.L.R. 2, at 7–8.
⁴⁷ [1983] A.C. 768 at 830–831 (Lord Diplock); 853 (Lord Brandon).
⁴⁸ [1983] 1 A.C. 768; see D. Oliver "The parties and Parliament: Representative or participatory democracy?" in Jeffrey Jowell and Dawn Oliver (eds.) *The Changing Constitution* at pp. 116–121.
⁴⁹ [1987] 3 All E.R. 671.
⁵⁰ *Ibid.* at 673.
⁵¹ *R.* v. *Sheffield City Council, ex p. Chadwick* (1986) 84 L.G.R. 563, D.C.; see also *R.* v. *Hackney London Borough Council* [1985] 1 W.L.R. 1229 where it was held that a councillor who belonged to a minority party on the council should not be excluded from attending sub-committee meetings and having access to papers if the council were satisfied, as they should have been in this case, that he had a "need to know" about the sub-committee's business. The sub-committee in question was concerned with policy and operational matters.
⁵² The Report of the Committee of Inquiry into the Conduct of Local Authority Business (the Widdicombe Report) recognising this problem, recommended that deliberative (i.e. policy-making) as opposed to decision-making, committees in local authorities could lawfully be composed of members of one party, but the Report sought to reduce the influence of non-elected party members by confining the right to vote on policy issues to elected members (Cmnd. 9797, 1986, at paras. 5.55, 6.69, 6.73, 6.79).
⁵³ *Padfield* v. *Minister of Agriculture, Fisheries and Food* [1968] A.C. 997.
⁵⁴ [1987] 2 All E.R. 671.
⁵⁵ at 675.
⁵⁶ *Ibid.* at 674.

[57] *Ibid.* at 676.
[58] [1925] A.C. 578, *per* Lord Atkinson.
[59] [1982] 2 W.L.R. at 69–70.
[60] [1985] 1 W.L.R. 298.
[61] [1987] 3 All E.R. 671, C.A.
[62] *Per* Sir John Donaldson, M.R. at 676.
[63] [1985] Q.B. 1153, D.C.
[64] *Ibid.* at 1176.
[65] [1985] Q.B. 1153, D.C.
[66] *Ibid.* at 1176.
[67] *Bushell* v. *Secretary of State for the Environment* [1981] A.C. 75, H.L.
[68] *Ibid.* at 122.
[69] *Ibid.* at 108.
[70] *Ibid.* at 100.
[71] *Ibid.* at 111.
[72] *Per* Lord Diplock at 98.
[73] *Per* Lord Diplock at 103.
[74] It will be recalled that the majority also had reservations about whether need was a matter of policy, although they treated it in the same way as policy—but for different reasons. Lord Lane stated that "The question of need is a matter of policy or so akin to a matter of policy that it was not for the inspector to make any recommendation." (at 123).
[75] Report of the Committee on Administrative Tribunals and Inquiries Cmnd. 218, para. 316. Lord Edmund-Davies at 46.
[76] *R.* v. *Secretary of State for Transport, ex p. Gwent County Council* [1987] 2 W.L.R. 961, C.A.

INDEX

Abuse of process, 6, 10, 20n.
Application for judicial review
    procedural exclusivity, 6, 9–12
    case load, 20n., 24
    conversion to writ action, 15
    See also Judicial review, Order 53.
Attorney-General, 14

BBC,
    whether a public authority, 2, 19n.,
        27–29

Civil Service Appeal Board, 2, 28
    whether subject to judicial review, 2
Collateral challenge, 12
Commercial decisions,
    not subject to judicial review, 2, 9, 28,
        33
Contract,
    not subject to judicial review, 2, 6, 7,
        9, 16, 19n., 28, 30
Contract compliance,
    judicial review, 1, 9, 19n.

Damages,
    jurisdiction to award, 5, 10
Decision-maker,
    conduct giving rise to legitimate
        expectation, 2, 38–43
Decision-making,
    subject to judicial review, 11
Declarations,
    jurisdiction to grant, 5, 10, 11, 15
Defence of the realm,
    not subject to judicial review, 2
Divisional Court,
    case load, 20n., 24
    popularity, 24
Domestic tribunals,
    judicial review of, 1, 6, 7, 27
    trade unions, 7

Employment,
    judicial review, 1, 2, 8, 33

European Community law,
    and proportionality, 3, 51, 52, 56–58
European Convention on Human
      Rights,
    and proportionality, 3, 51, 58–59
Executive functions,
    not subject to judicial review, 11

Foreign affairs,
    not subject to judicial review, 2
French law,
    and proportionality, 3, 51, 54–56

German law,
    and proportionality, 3, 51, 52–54

Injunctions,
    jurisdiction to grant, 5, 10
Interests,
    affected by policy, 3, 77
    protected by judicial review, 2, 37–49,
        77
Irrationality,
    a ground for judicial review, 7

Judicial review,
    abuse of power, 47–48
    abuse of process, 6, 10, 20n.
    alternative remedies, 18n.
    arbitrators not subject to, 27
    boundaries of, 1, 5–17
    breach of natural justice, 8, 13, 59
    Civil Service Appeal Board, 2
    collateral challenge, 11, 12
    commercial decisions, 2, 9, 28, 33
    contract, 2, 6, 7, 9, 16, 19n., 28, 30
    contract compliance, 1, 9, 19n.
    cross-examination, 3, 10, 86–88
    defence of the realm, 2
    discovery, 10
    discretion to refuse, 2
    dismissal, whether subject to, 8
    domestic tribunals, 1, 6, 7, 27
    employment, 1, 2, 8, 33